Redemption

A Fundamental Doctrine of the Book of Mormon

John Sroka

Redemption by John J. Sroka

First Edition, First Printing of 2,000 Hardbound Copies, 2004
Publisher: Granite Publishing
Orem, Utah

Cover Art by: Greg K. Olsen

Cover design by: Steve Gray

ISBN: 1-932280-66-9
Library of Congress Control Number: 2004114845
Printed in the United States of America

To three missionaries
who served in the California North Mission
in 1967 and 1968

Joe Shumway
Ken Asay
Eric Hazelle

Also to two missionaries
who served in the New England Mission
in 1971

Art Bingham
Randy Browning

My wife and I will be forever grateful
for their message and testimony of
Jesus Christ.

Contents

Foreword

How beautiful upon the mountains
are the feet of him that bringeth good tidings,
that publisheth peace;
that bringeth good tidings of good,
that publisheth salvation;
that saith unto Zion,
Thy God reigneth!
(Isaiah 52:7)

Doing the Research Myself

I have written the book that I wanted to read. I kept going to libraries and bookstores, searching for a book that did not exist. I finally decided that the only way to get the information that I sought was to do the research myself. I wanted to know why there were certain redundancies in the Book of Mormon. I knew there were patterns to those redundancies, and after reading the Book of Mormon many times, I realized that those patterns were connected to the doctrine of redemption.

As I began this work, I felt that I should write a chapter to introduce my reader to the Book of Mormon. I wanted to give another view. Much has been written about how the Prophet Joseph Smith translated the Book of Mormon. What needed to be written was the other half—how Mormon and Moroni put together the plates from which the Book of Mormon was translated. I had my first chapter.

As I began my research on redemption, I found that the doctrine of redemption was tied to other doctrines. The word "redemption" is not just a broad, generic term. At times it has a specific meaning. I had my second chapter. The following three chapters are also about redemption. They contain three of the redemptive patterns found in the Book of Mormon. Much has been written about the atonement, but little about redemption.

The appendix of this book has only one part. It contains a research paper on dating the Book of Mormon—my attempt to date each verse.

This book is not meant to be comprehensive. It is not the final word on anything. I have added numerous notes to each chapter. Their intent is not to convert readers to my way of thinking. They only exhibit my line of thinking.

I am a student of the Book of Mormon. The purpose of this book is to get readers to go back to the Book of Mormon and rediscover its depth. I believe that the Book of Mormon is the word of God. I believe that there are many marvelous and wonderful things for each of us to discover within its pages.

Acknowledgments

I especially wish to thank my wife and children for their support, patience and sacrifice as I have researched and written this work. I also wish to thank Don Norton for his willingness to read and edit my manuscripts as they went through several drafts.

CHAPTER 1

An Introduction to the Book of Mormon

And thou hast made us
that we could write but little,
because of the awkwardness of our hands.
(Ether 12:24)

The Writing of the Book of Mormon

Since the publication of the Book of Mormon in 1830, enemies of the Church have attempted to explain it away with every possible theory, yet it stands inviolate to their attempts. Within the pages of the Book of Mormon, prophets of God describe how it came forth.

In this account I will not theorize, but will go directly to the Book of Mormon and see what it has to say for itself. First will be an assessment of the source materials Mormon and Moroni had at their disposal. Then there will be a review of the lives of these two prophets who labored to complete the Book of Mormon to see if we can discover when the Book of Mormon was written.

Source Material of the Book of Mormon

The Book of Mormon was not written in a vacuum. Both Mormon and Moroni used a number of source documents, and they were forthright about their sources. Mormon's abridgment came from the large plates of Nephi. He later finished his portion of the Book of Mormon by adding the small plates of Nephi. Moroni abridged the plates of Ether, and later included materials from both the time of Christ and his own time.

The small plates and the large plates of Nephi cite other sources. For example, the small plates contain passages from the plates of brass, and the large plates contain the record of Zeniff. Thus it becomes important to review each of the Nephite records mentioned in the Book of Mormon and determine their roles in its writing.

Plates of Brass

Nephi obtained the plates of brass from Jerusalem about 600 B.C. (1 Nephi 4:24). They contained the holy scriptures from the beginning, to the commencement of the reign of king Zedekiah (Alma 37:3; 1 Nephi 5:11-12). The impact of the plates of brass on the Nephite culture was huge. After searching them, Lehi knew he was a descendant of Joseph (1 Nephi 5:10-14). He taught his children from these plates (Mosiah 1:4). They contained the law and the prophecies of the holy prophets down to the time Lehi left Jerusalem (1 Nephi 4:16; Mosiah 2:34). Through them the memory of the people was enlarged, and many were "convinced of the error of their ways" and brought to "the knowledge of their God unto the salvation of their souls" (Alma 37:8).

The Lord instructed Nephi to create the small plates for the instruction of his people (1 Nephi 19:3). The small plates contained many large passages from the plates of brass; quotes from those plates are found throughout the

Book of Mormon. It should not be surprising that Nephite prophets taught from these plates, for they contained the holy scriptures (2 Nephi 4:15). Each quote reveals the Nephites' love and respect of the scriptures, and the huge impact of the plates of brass on the Nephite culture.

Plates of Nephi

Nephi began keeping a record of his people shortly after their arrival in the promised land, about 590 B.C. (1 Nephi 18:23-19:1). Twenty years later he was commanded to make another set of plates (2 Nephi 5:30). This smaller set was to have a special purpose, which was to contain the more plain and precious parts of the ministry and prophecies, to be kept for the instruction of the people (1 Nephi 19:3). The first and larger set of plates was to contain the reign of the kings and the history of the wars and contentions of the people (1 Nephi 9:2-4). This division of purpose started about 570 B.C. and was discontinued sometime before the end of the reign of king Benjamin.

We know a great deal about the small plates of Nephi. After Mormon completed his abridgment of the large plates, he took from[1] the small plates what have become the first six books of the Book of Mormon: First Nephi, Second Nephi,[2] Jacob, Enos, Jarom, Omni.

Nephi called both of his sets of plates the plates of Nephi (1 Nephi 9:2). It was his brother Jacob who first differentiated them by their size.[3] The large plates of Nephi must have been substantially bigger than the small plates. The large plates of Nephi in their abridged form are more than three and a half times the size of the small plates in their unabridged form.[4]

Plates of Ether

The plates of Ether were found by a small number of king Limhi's men as they searched for the land of Zarahemla in 121 B.C. (Mosiah 21:25-27). This record contained the history of the Jaredite people, an earlier nation that had been destroyed.[5] Mosiah translated the plates sometime between 121 and 91 B.C. (Mosiah 28:11, 17). The account Mosiah gave to his people was incomplete. He kept back the details of the vision of the brother of Jared (Ether 4:1), and the Jaredite secret plans, oaths, and covenants (Alma 37:29). Mormon intended that this partial account be added to the Book of Mormon (Mosiah 28:19). This was not completed in his lifetime, but his son Moroni later abridged the plates of Ether.

Moroni stated that his abridgment of the Book of Ether was taken from the twenty-four plates found by the people of Limhi (Ether 1:2; 15:33-34). He added that to read from the writings of the brother of Jared was overpowering (Ether 12:24). Moroni explained that because of his weakness in writing, he wrote only a few things, not even a hundredth part of what Ether had written (Ether 12:40; 15:33). Even as he was abridging the Book of Ether, Moroni recorded, "I am commanded that I should hide [the plates of Ether] up again in the earth."[6] The logical assumption is that the book of Ether and the sealed portion of the Book of Mormon were both taken from the plates of Ether.

Why did Moroni go directly to the plates of Ether and not to Mosiah's translation? Moroni was commanded to write the very things which the brother of Jared saw (Ether 4:4-5), a vision that had been excluded from Mosiah's translation (Ether 4:1). Moroni thus had to use the plates of Ether to write these things.

After spending years translating and engraving the brother of Jared's vision of the beginning of the world to the ending thereof, Moroni wrote, "Jesus Christ hath shown you unto me, and I know your doings" (Mormon 8:27-35). Moroni had not only become familiar with the plates of Ether, he had also become familiar with our day and our "doings." This preparation enabled Moroni to address specifically the needs of the people of our day as he abridged the plates of Ether.[7]

Moroni's writings bear a strong second witness to many of the things his father had taught and recorded.

Other Records

Record of Lehi

First Nephi contains only a small portion of Lehi's writings. Nephi began the small plates by abridging the record of his father (1 Nephi 1:17). He had already preserved the unabridged version of this record upon the large plates (1 Nephi 10:15; 19:1-2). The record of Lehi was also called the Book of Lehi.[8]

Plates or Record of Zeniff

Chapters nine through twenty-two of Mosiah contain the record of Zeniff, which had originally been a separate set of plates.[9] It is an account of a group of Nephites who went back to the land of Nephi to inherit the land of their fathers (Mosiah 9:3). That was their right. Their fathers had possessed the land of Nephi for almost four centuries. Why should they have to start all over again in the land of Zarahemla?

The account ends generations later with a humbler and wiser group of Nephites, happy to become the subjects of the righteous king Mosiah in the land of Zarahemla (Mosiah 22:13).

Records from the Land Northward

Mormon noted that the people kept many records while they were in the land northward, records that were "particular and very large" (Helaman 3:10-13).

The Hundredth Part

Mormon lamented that he could not write the hundredth part of the doings of his people (Words of Mormon 1:5). This statement and others like it lead one to ask: How many records were there? Brigham Young said there were "wagon loads."[10] These were sacred records. Mormon noted in his abridgment of the large plates of Nephi that he had not written even a hundredth part of the things which Jesus had taught the people (3 Nephi 26:6-7). He also referred to other records from the time of Christ (3 Nephi 5:9; 8:2, 19). As with other early Christian libraries, we are left to imagine what the contents were.

Timeline

The Book of Mormon is an abridgment of the writings of many men who had the spirit of prophecy and of revelation. Mormon and Moroni were called to be the historians and abridgers of those sacred records. When the events of their lives are placed into a timeline, we realize that war between the Nephites and the Lamanites was not a continuous series of battles. There were long periods of peace during which the Nephites chose not to repent. We begin to question. When was Mormon born? At what age did he begin to write the Book of Mormon? How long did it take to complete? When were the Nephites destroyed? It becomes clear that Mormon and Moroni wanted their readers to know when things happened.

Mormon

A.D. 311
Mormon was born.[11]

321 (Mormon 1:2-5)
Ammaron went to the hill Shim and deposited the sacred records (4 Nephi 1:48-49). Ammaron then revealed their location to Mormon and called him to be the next historian.[12]

322 (Mormon 1:6-12)
Mormon's father took him from the land northward[13] into the land southward to the land of Zarahemla. After almost three centuries of peace, war began in the borders of Zarahemla by the waters of Sidon.[14] There were a number of battles in which the Nephites were victorious, and the Lamanites withdrew.

322-326 (Mormon 1:12-14)
There was peace in the land for about four years. Wickedness prevailed insomuch that the three disciples of the Lord were taken away, and miracles and healing ceased.

326 (Mormon 1:15-2:2)
Mormon was visited of the Lord, and he tasted and knew of the goodness of Jesus. He was forbidden to preach to the Nephites, for they had willfully rebelled against God.

Because of the hardness of their hearts the land was cursed for their sake. Gadianton robbers infested the land, and the inhabitants hid their treasures in the earth. Sorcery, witchcraft, and magic were practiced throughout the land. War began again, and Mormon was appointed the leader of the Nephite armies.

A.D. 327-330 (Mormon 2:3-9)
The Lamanites came upon the Nephites who began to retreat toward the north countries. The Nephites were driven from the land of Zarahemla to the city of Angola, from Angola to the land of David, and from David to the land of Joshua. The Nephites gathered together into one body. They did not repent. The Lamanite army came against them and was defeated.

331-344 (Mormon 2:10-15)
The Nephites began to repent, but their repentance was incomplete, for "they did not come unto Jesus with broken hearts and contrite spirits." The Nephites remained in the land of Joshua.

335 (Mormon 2:17-19)[15]
Mormon went to the hill Shim and took possession of the large plates of Nephi. In 321 Ammaron had commanded Mormon to take these plates when he became twenty-four years old, and engrave on them all the things he observed concerning his people (Mormon 1:3-4).

345 (Mormon 2:16, 20-21)
The Nephites fled before the Lamanites from Joshua to the land of Jashon (near the hill Shim), and from Jashon to the land of Shem, where they gathered in as many of their people as possible to save them from destruction.

A.D. 346-349 (Mormon 2:22-28)
The Lamanites began to come upon the Nephites. Mormon spoke to his people, quoting parts of the title of liberty.[16] He urged them to stand boldly and "fight for their wives, and their children, and their houses, and their homes." The Nephites withstood the Lamanites with such firmness that they fled, and the Nephites pursued them until they had again taken possession of the lands of their inheritance. This was a great victory for the Nephites. Mormon had delivered them from the Lamanites.

350 (Mormon 2:28-29)
A treaty was made and the lands were divided. The Lamanites gave the Nephites the land northward. The Nephites gave the Lamanites all the land southward.

350-360 (Mormon 3:1-3)
The Lamanites did not come to battle for ten years. Mormon employed his people in preparation for the next time of battle. Mormon was commanded by the Lord to begin his ministry, but the Nephites hardened their hearts. This is the most likely time for Mormon's sermon on faith, hope, and charity (see Moroni 7).

360 (Mormon 3:4-6)
The king of the Lamanites sent an epistle to Mormon making known their preparations for battle. Mormon gathered his people to the land Desolation[17] by the narrow pass, to stop the Lamanites from gaining possession of any of their lands.

A.D. 361 (Mormon 3:7)
The Lamanites came to the city of Desolation to battle against the Nephites. The Nephites beat them, and they returned to their own lands.

362 (Mormon 3:8-22)
The Lamanites came to battle and were defeated again. This was the third time Mormon had delivered his people out of the hands of their enemies, yet they had not repented. Because of the Nephites' great victory, they boasted of their own strength and swore forbidden oaths. Mormon refused to have any part of their plans for vengeance and relinquished his command of the Nephite armies. Mormon turned his attention to the future: he wrote to the Gentiles, the house of Israel, the Lamanites, and all the ends of the earth. It was at this time that Mormon began his abridgment of the large plates of Nephi.[18]

363 (Mormon 4:1-6)
The Nephites went into Lamanite lands to battle.[19] The Nephites were driven back to the land of Desolation, and from Desolation to the city Teancum. The Lamanites made preparations to come against Teancum.

364-366 (Mormon 4:7-10)
The Lamanites came against the city Teancum but were driven back. When the Nephites saw that they were stronger than the Lamanites, they retook the city Desolation. Thousands had been slain on both sides.

367 (Mormon 4:10-15)
The Lamanites came upon the Nephites to battle. The Nephites had not repented. The Lamanites, outnumbering the Nephites, took possession of the city Desolation.

The Lamanites marched against the city Teancum, and it was also lost. Many Nephite women and children were taken prisoner and sacrificed to Lamanite idol gods. This angered the Nephites, who drove the Lamanites out of their lands.

A.D. 367-375 (Mormon 4:16)
The Lamanites remained in their own lands. This was a period of peace.

375-379 (Mormon 4:17-5:5)
The Lamanites came against the Nephites with all their might. The Nephites were overwhelmed and driven from the city Desolation to the city Boaz. As the Nephites were being driven from Boaz to the city of Jordan, Mormon saw that the Lamanites were about to overthrow the land. He went to the hill Shim and took possession of all the sacred records. The tide of the war had changed for the Nephites from offensive to defensive. They had sought vengeance, but had been beaten and driven (Mormon 4:1-5). As the Nephites retreated, they could gain no power over the Lamanites. Mormon, willing to assist the Nephites, was given command of their armies. Mormon, however, was without hope, for he knew the judgments of God would come upon the Nephites, who had not repented. Even so, when the Lamanites came against the city of Jordan, they were repulsed twice. A new defensive front[20] had been achieved. The Nephites, who had not been gathered in as their armies passed through their lands were destroyed by the Lamanites, and their towns, villages, and cities were burned.

A.D. 379-380
This is the most likely time for Mormon's first epistle to his son Moroni (see Moroni 8).

380-384 (Mormon 5:6-6:5)
The Lamanites came once more against the Nephites. The Nephites were outnumbered; their defensive line was broken and they retreated. This is probably when Mormon wrote his second epistle to his son Moroni (see Moroni 9).[21] Mormon abridged his writing from the large plates of Nephi, which he had written. Those writings have become the first five chapters of Mormon.[22] Mormon wrote to the king of the Lamanites of his desire to gather his people to the land of Cumorah, and there give them battle. His request was granted. Mormon marched his armies to Cumorah and gathered in the remainder of his people.[23]

385 (Mormon 6:5-22)
Mormon knew this would be the last struggle of his people. He hid up in the hill Cumorah all the sacred records except for his abridgement, which he gave to his son Moroni. The Lamanite armies came against the Nephites to battle. The Lamanites greatly outnumbered the Nephites, whose armies were hewn down. Mormon was wounded and left for dead. There were only twenty-four Nephite survivors, Moroni being among them. Mormon added to his abridgement what have become chapters six and seven of Mormon, in which he lamented, "O ye fair ones, how could ye have departed from the ways of the Lord! O ye fair ones how could ye have rejected that Jesus, who stood with open arms to receive you! … O that ye had repented before this great destruction had come upon you." He wrote the Words of Mormon and added the small plates of Nephi to his abridgment. He returned[24] the plates to

his son Moroni and called him as the next historian, charging him to write somewhat concerning Christ (Words of Mormon 1:1-6). It is assumed that Mormon died in this year. He had been a prolific writer, and his writings ceased.

Moroni

A.D. 385-401

As Mormon delivered the plates to his son Moroni, he prayed for three things: 1) that Moroni may survive the Nephites; 2) that Moroni write somewhat concerning the Nephites and somewhat concerning Christ; 3) that perhaps some day this record may profit the remnant of this people (Words of Mormon 1:2). These words were most likely written shortly after the last great battle in 385. Moroni did not begin to write the eighth chapter of Mormon until 401 (Mormon 8:6). Why had Moroni waited sixteen years before fulfilling the wishes of his father? What was he doing between 385 and 401 that was more important than fulfilling the last request of his father? Moroni explains that the Lord had commanded him to write the very things which the brother of Jared saw, and seal them up with the interpreters (Ether 4:4-5). The Lord had shown the brother of Jared all the inhabitants of the earth which had been and would be, even to the ends of the earth (Ether 3:25). Nephi foretold that the sealed book shall contain a revelation from God, from the beginning of the world to the ending thereof (2 Nephi 27:7). To translate and write such a revelation would have been a tremendous undertaking, perhaps twice the size of his father's work,[25] and may have taken sixteen years to complete. Mormon had written of his intention to add Mosiah's translation of the plates of Ether to his abridgement

(Mosiah 28:17-19), but this was not completed in his lifetime. Moroni may have read these verses and inquired of the Lord, before being commanded to write the vision of brother of Jared.

A.D. 401

After writing and sealing up the brother of Jared's vision, Moroni fulfilled his father's commandments by writing what is now chapters eight and nine of Mormon (Mormon 8:1). Moroni recorded the sad tale of the destruction of his people (Mormon 8:2-13). He wrote somewhat concerning Christ, specifically addressing those who do not believe in him (Mormon 9:1-29). Moroni also wrote to the people of our time concerning the coming forth of the Book of Mormon (Mormon 8:14-41; 9:30-37). Having spent years translating from the twenty-four plates, abridging the Book of Ether would have been a comparatively easy task, and was likely completed that year.[26] Moroni then wrote the title page of the Book of Mormon. The plates of Ether were returned to the place of the Nephite sacred records (Ether 4:3). The plates of Mormon were placed in the hill Cumorah (Mormon 8:4, 14).

401-421

Moroni believed his work had been completed (Moroni 1:1) and that it did not matter where he went (Mormon 8:4). After completing the sealed portion of the Book of Mormon, Moroni would have known of the future restoration of the gospel and the trials of the early Latter-day Saints. What does a prophet do when he believes his work is done? Where did Moroni go during this twenty-year period of time? Although these questions cannot be answered with certainty, it should be noted that some of the early Latter-day Saints believed that Moroni had dedicated temple sites at Kirtland, Jackson County, Nauvoo, St. George, and Manti.[27] Moroni said simply, "I wander whithersoever I can for the safety of mine own life" (Moroni 1:3).

A.D. 421
Moroni returned to Cumorah and wrote the Book of Moroni. After writing a four-verse introduction, he recorded the words that Jesus Christ had spoken to the twelve Nephite disciples when he gave them power to give the Holy Ghost. This satisfied another element Mormon had intended to add to his abridgement (3 Nephi 18:37). Moroni may have read this verse and then searched through the sacred Nephite records, finding "a few more things" (Moroni 1:4) to add to his record. The plates were returned to the hill Cumorah (Moroni 10:2).

With the destruction of the Nephites, there was no one to continue their sacred record or to record the death of Moroni. Some of the early Latter-day Saints believed the Lamanites killed Moroni.[28]

Summary

Mormon's portion of the Book of Mormon was accomplished between 362 and 385, a period of twenty-three years. This latter part of his life can be broken down into three distinct time periods.

A.D. 362-375
Mormon had relinquished his command of the Nephite armies and turned his attention to abridging the large plates

of Nephi. The largest portion of his abridgment would have been completed during this time period.

A.D. 375-380

Mormon took possession of all the sacred records.[29] His command of the Nephite armies was reinstated. The Nephites created a new defensive front and repulsed the Lamanites twice. Mormon had weighty military responsibilities during the latter years of this time period.[30]

380-385

The Nephite defensive line was broken. Mormon successfully petitioned the king of the Lamanites and was granted his desire to gather his people to the land of Cumorah for battle. This time of gathering was a time of peace. Mormon may have worked at a frantic pace[31] to complete his abridgment. The first seven chapters of Mormon were abridged and written during this time period.

What did it take to write the Book of Mormon?

- It took many holy men of God who had the spirit of prophecy and of revelation.
- It involved millenniums of sacred historical records.
- It took about twenty-five years to abridge these records into a single volume.[32]
- It required a comprehensive knowledge of Egyptian and a reformed Egyptian dialect.
- It took the gift and power of God to translate the ancient language of the Jaredites.

The Book of Mormon was not the product of one man; it was the product of a nation. Generations of Nephite historians kept the sacred records of their people. Some of these historians also collected the sacred records of other nations. The plates of brass, or record of the Jews, became one of the foundation stones of the Nephite culture. The plates of Ether, or the record of the Jaredites, warns every nation that possesses the land of promise that they shall serve God, or they shall be swept off (Ether 2:8-12). The words of the prophets of ancient America were recorded. As Mormon and Moroni abridged the sacred records of the Nephite and Jaredite nations, they were in the mature years of their lives.[33] They hoped to convince the people of our day that Jesus is the Christ, the Eternal God, manifesting himself unto all nations.

Notes

[1] Mormon wrote, "I shall take these plates [which I shall *take from* the (small) plates of Nephi] and put them with the remainder of my [abridged] record" (Words of Mormon 1:5-6). Mormon did not write I shall *take* the plates of Nephi; instead he wrote I shall *take from* the plates of Nephi. This indicates that he may have made a copy of the small plates of Nephi to put with his abridgment of the large plates. But if he meant "copy," why did he not write the word "copy"? This word is not found in the Book of Mormon. There may not have been an equivalent word in their reformed Egyptian language. Mormon may have meant "copy" when he wrote, "take from."

There are other indications that the small plates may have been copied in the prefaces of the books of First Nephi, Second Nephi, and Jacob. Most of the text of these three books was written in the first person, but the prefaces were written in the third person. This indicates that another person other than Nephi or Jacob may have written them. Mormon is credited with writing the prefaces of the books of Alma, Helaman, and Third Nephi, which were also written in third person.

Another indication that the small plates may have been copied can be found in the first verse of the second chapter of Jacob. It is missing the typical "I, Jacob" signature. While the text around this verse was written in the first person, this verse is written in the third person. It may be an editorial note made by Mormon as he copied the small plates of Nephi.

It should not be surprising that Mormon may have made a copy of the small plates of Nephi to attach to his abridgment. He noted that the plates were "handed down from king Benjamin, from generation to generation until they have fallen into my hands. And I, Mormon, pray to God that they may be preserved from this time henceforth. And I know they will be preserved; for there are great things written upon them, out of which my people and their brethren shall be judged at the great and last day, according to the word of God which is written" (Words of Mormon 1:11). Mormon knew the plates were to be preserved. The Nephites would be judged out of these books (2 Nephi 29:11; 3 Nephi 27:25-26). Mormon would not have taken the chance that these records might fall into the hands of those who would destroy them (Mormon 6:6). Their preservation was crucial, and the small plates of Nephi were no exception to that rule (Jacob 1:3).

[2] The writings of Nephi were divided into two books: the First Book of Nephi, and the Second Book of Nephi. He began the small plates by abridging what had been written on the large plates (1 Nephi 1:17). The subtitle "his reign and his ministry" for First Nephi makes perfect sense because Nephi was the king at the time he began engraving the small plates (2 Nephi 5:18, 30).

Whereas First Nephi contains a great deal of the history of the people, Second Nephi contains almost none. The Second Book of Nephi contains exhortations, blessings, sermons, prophecies, and testimonies. This leads one to surmise that Second Nephi may be the beginning of the unabridged "more plain and precious parts of the ministry." This conclusion has only one major problem: The first five chapters of Second Nephi contain events that occurred prior to the creation of the small plates (2 Nephi 5:30).

There is a relatively simple explanation to this problem. After Nephi was commanded to "make other plates" he likely would not have duplicated any of his writings, because of the difficulty of engraving on plates. If Nephi had gotten behind with engraving, years behind, that could explain why the first five chapters became a part of Second Nephi and not First Nephi.

What possible explanations could there be for Nephi to put off engraving the large plates for such an extended period of time?

1) Nephi did not indicate how often he engraved upon the large plates. It may have been normal for him to write on some type of temporary material for years before updating these plates.

2) With Lehi's death, the rebellion of Nephi's brethren, and his departure into the wilderness, Nephi may have gotten behind with his engraving of the large plates. Nephi and his people built a new city, planted and harvested crops, made swords for their defense, and built a temple. During this period of time, Nephi may have had other priorities.

3) It may have taken years for the Nephites to find another source of gold in the land of Nephi to produce more plates.

If this theory were true, it would mean that the first part of the lost 116-page manuscript, which contains the same period of time as First Nephi, would be very similar to First Nephi. They both would be abridged from the same portion of the large plates. On the other hand, the contents of the latter part of the lost 116-page manuscript would be very different, for it would be an abridgment of the reign of the kings and the history of the people, which are recorded only in an abbreviated form from the beginning of Second Nephi through the end of Omni.

[3] Jacob was the first to refer to the plates of Nephi, which contained the more plain and precious parts of the ministry and prophecies as "the small plates" (Jacob 1:1). Jacob recorded that Nephi had instructed him to "*preserve* these plates *and hand them down unto my seed, from generation to generation*" (Jacob 1:3). The small plates remained with Jacob's family until Amaleki, who, "having no seed, and knowing king Benjamin to be a just man before the Lord," delivered the plates to him (Omni 1:25).

Jacob was the first to refer to the plates of Nephi, which contained the reign of the kings and the history of the people as "the larger plates" (Jacob 3:13). Nephi recorded that the Lord God promised him that these plates "shall be kept and *preserved, and handed down unto my seed, from generation to generation*" (2 Nephi 25:21; see also 1 Nephi 13:35, 41). The large plates were "handed down by the kings, from generation to generation until the days of king Benjamin" (Words of Mormon 1:10). Mormon confirmed, "The kingdom had been conferred upon none but those who were descendants of Nephi" (Mosiah 25:13). King Mosiah had no one to confer the kingdom on, for none of his sons would accept the kingdom (Mosiah 28:10). Therefore he conferred upon Alma, who was the son of Alma, all the things that had been kept (Mosiah 28:11-20). Alma was a descendant of Nephi (Mosiah 17:2).

Alma attempted to confer the records and the sacred things upon Nephihah (Alma 50:38). Alma may have felt that since the kings had handed down these things, they should now be handed down through the chief judges. Nephihah refused to take possession of those records; therefore, Alma conferred them upon his son Helaman (Alma 50:38). The large plates remained with Alma's family until Ammaron, who, "being constrained by the Holy Ghost," hid up the records (4 Nephi 1:48). He then went to Mormon and revealed to him their location and called him to be the next historian. Mormon was also a descendant of Nephi (Mormon 1:2-5; 8:13).

[4] The printer's manuscript of the Book of Mormon, from Mosiah through the seventh chapter of Mormon, is on 306 pages of foolscap paper. Adding back the 116 pages of the lost manuscript sums up to 422 pages of foolscap. Therefore the large plates of Nephi in their abridged form were on about 422 pages of foolscap paper.

The printer's manuscript of the Book of Mormon, from First Nephi though Omni (the small plates), was written on 115 pages of foolscap. Therefore the large plates of Nephi in their abridged form are 3.67 times the size of the small plates in their unabridged form. The large plates of Nephi in their unabridged state must be massive. Once these plates became too large and cumbersome for one person to carry, they probably were divided into volumes (Leland H. Monson, "Mormon," *Improvement Era*, Sep. 1945, 551). No one ever said that the large plates of Nephi were contained within a single volume of plates.

[5] The Jaredites were not of the house of Israel (Hugh Nibley, *Lehi in the Desert and the World of the Jaredites* (1952), 265). The promise of a continuation of seed was not theirs. The splendor of their account is found in the experience of the brother of Jared. From it we learn that through faith in Christ, the great blessings that can be ours.

[6] Some have supposed that the first three verses of the fourth chapter of Ether refer to the plates of Mormon. There is no indication that the plates of Mormon had been placed in the earth before this time. Thus they could not be hid up again in the earth, whereas all the other sacred records (including the plates of Ether) had been hid up in the hill Cumorah in the year 385 by Mormon (Mormon 6:6). The first three verses of the fourth chapter of Ether are all about the plates of Ether. "Mosiah kept *them* (the plates of Ether, which contained the things that the brother of Jared had seen) that they should not come unto the world.... Therefore I am commanded that I should hide *them* (the plates of Ether) up again in the earth" (Ether 4:1, 3). The plates of Mormon are not mentioned until the fourth verse.

[7] The Book of Ether contains messages specifically directed to the people of our time. Chapters two, four, five, eight, and twelve contain editorial notes, written to the people of our day by the prophet Moroni. Ezra Taft Benson taught that Mormon also wrote for our time: "Under the inspiration of God, who sees all things from the beginning, [Mormon] abridged centuries of records, choosing the stories, speeches, and events that would be most helpful to us" (Ezra Taft Benson, *A Witness and a Warning* (1988), 19).

[8] In the preface of the first addition of the Book of Mormon, Joseph Smith wrote, "I translated, by the gift and power of God, and caused to be written, one hundred and sixteen pages, the which I took from the Book of Lehi, which was an account abridged from the

plates of Lehi, by the hand of Mormon." Some have asked: Was the Book of Lehi taken from the plates of Lehi or the plates of Nephi? The answer is both. The plates of Lehi were part of the large plates of Nephi, just as the plates of Jacob were part of the small plates of Nephi (Jacob 3:14). In other words, just as the portion of the small plates of Nephi that contained the Book of Jacob could be referred to as the plates of Jacob, the portion of the large plates of Nephi that contained the Book of Lehi were referred to as the plates of Lehi (David E. Sloan, "The Book of Lehi and the Plates of Lehi," *Journal of the Book of Mormon*, 6 (Fall 1997): 270-271). The large plates of Nephi were also referred to as the "book of Nephi," from which Mormon had taken all the account he had written (Helaman 2:14).

[9] The record of Zeniff was originally a separate set of plates (Mosiah 8:5), which causes one to ask: Was Mormon's account of this record taken from the plates of Zeniff or the large plates of Nephi? After abridging the Book of Mosiah, Mormon noted that he had taken from the book (or large plates) of Nephi all the account that he had written (Helaman 2:14). We can safely assume that the record of Zeniff had been added to the Book of Mosiah. In this case the plates of Zeniff had become a part of the large plates of Nephi, afterwards referred to as the record of Zeniff.

[10] *Journal of Discourses*, 19:38.

[11] Mormon was about ten years of age in 321 when Ammaron hid up the records (4 Nephi 1:48; Mormon 1:2). In the year 326 Mormon was fifteen. (Mormon 1:15-2:2). Thus Mormon was born about 311.

[12] Ammaron was over a hundred years old when he hid the sacred records. It is doubtful that a man of his age and time would have traveled far to hide the plates, or to call Mormon as the next historian. The early years of Mormon's life most likely took place near the hill Shim, in the land northward.

[13] The Nephites talked of either the land southward or the land northward. It was always an either-or situation. Mormon's statement that he was carried into the land southward implies that he was carried from the land northward.

[14] Mormon's father moved to Zarahemla in the same year that war began "in the borders of Zarahemla, by the waters of Sidon" (Mormon 1:10). Was this "dumb luck," or was it purposeful? Was Mormon's father in the Nephite military, called to an area where things were heating up? Did Mormon's father leave other

family members behind in the land northward where it was safe? Could this explain how Mormon was able to "go forth at the head of an army of the Nephites" when he was only in his sixteenth year? Had Mormon's father tutored him in the military arts from a very early age?

[15] Verses seventeen through nineteen of the second chapter of Mormon are an editorial note. In the preceding verse (sixteen), Mormon starts writing the events of the year 345. In verse seventeen he begins his editorial note by referring back to when he was twenty-four years old (in 335) when he had gone to the hill Shim to take the plates of Nephi. In verses eighteen and nineteen he continues his editorial note. Mormon relates that on the plates of Nephi he "did make a full account of all the wickedness," but that on the plates of Mormon he "did forbear to make a full account of their wickedness." Mormon later recorded that his account of "the wickedness of this people" had been abridged between 380 and 384 (Mormon 5:9). Verse twenty begins with "And it came to pass," signaling that his editorial note had ended and that he was continuing with the events of the year 345.

[16] General Moroni's title of liberty was "in memory of our God, our religion, and freedom, and our peace, our wives, and our children" (Alma 46:12). Mormon must have found that his people had fallen to a point where they were not longer inspired by God, religion, freedom and peace. Therefore he urged them with the more temporal, house and homes.

[17] The cities of Desolation and Teancum were not mentioned before the year 360; they may have been built between 350 and 360 as Mormon prepared the Nephite lands for the next "time of battle" (Mormon 3:1).

[18] Sidney B. Sperry published his "conclusion that Mormon began his work of abridging about A.D. 362 and completed his writing A.D. 384." He did not consider the sixth and seventh chapters of Mormon to be abridged. Sperry pointed out that Mormon's abridgment "would doubtless not be made until long after A.D. 334." His major point was that in 362 (Mormon 3:17-19), after Mormon had utterly refused to be a commander and leader of his people, he addressed himself to the "Gentiles," to the "house of Israel," and to the "remnant of this people" (Sidney B. Sperry, *Book of Mormon Chronology* (1970), 32-33). The Book of Mormon begins with a similar statement, that it is "written to the Lamanites,

who are a remnant of the house of Israel; and also to Jew and Gentile" (Title page of the Book of Mormon).

19 "The Nephites did go up…to battle against the Lamanites, out of the land Desolation" (Mormon 4:1). During the treaty of 350, the Nephites were given the land northward, even to the narrow pass that led into the land southward (Mormon 2:28-29). The land Desolation was in the borders, by the narrow pass (Mormon 3:5). For the Nephites to go out of the land Desolation against the Lamanites, they would have had to go into Lamanite lands. Mormon commented that because of this, the Nephites began to be smitten (Mormon 4:4). Gidgiddoni had taught his people the same principle (3 Nephi 3:21).

20 Mormon noted, "there were also other cities, …which strongholds did cut [the Lamanites] off that they could not get into the country which lay before us, to destroy the inhabitants of our land" (Mormon 5:4). The military term is a "defensive front."

21 Mormon wrote his first epistle soon after his son had been called to the ministry (Moroni 8:1). In it he promised, "I will write again" (Moroni 8:27). Mormon began his second epistle by stating, "I write unto you again" (Moroni 9:1). These epistles were not years apart. They mention each other. They were a pair.

Mormon served in the military at two different times: first, from 326 to 362; second, from about 375 to 385. It is difficult to believe that Mormon's epistles are from the first period. Mormon wrote in his second epistle of the Nephite's thirst for blood and revenge (Moroni 9:5, 23). Mormon had left the military in 362 because of the Nephites' plan for vengeance (Mormon 3:9-11). It is also difficult to believe that Moroni would have been old enough to be called to the ministry until some time after the first period.

When we review the second period, from the time Mormon took command of the armies, for "a sore battle" in which the Nephites "did not conquer" (Moroni 9:2), we find only two. First, the battle that started in 380 (Mormon 5:6-7). The second was the last great battle in 385. Mormon and Moroni were together at Cumorah. Because only twenty-four Nephites survived the last great battle, it is difficult to believe that Mormon's second epistle was written at that late date (Moroni 9:3, 17, 22-24). This epistle was most likely written shortly after the battle that started in 380.

22 Mormon wrote a *small* abridgment of *the things he had seen*, daring not to give a full account of the wickedness of his people, that we "might not have too great sorrow" (Mormon 5:9). This

small record of the things he had seen or observed concerning his people (Mormon 1:4) starts with the first verse of the first chapter of Mormon, where he wrote, "And now I, Mormon, make a record of *the things which I have* both *seen* and heard."

[23] Gathering the remaining Nephites may have taken years. It took four years for the Jaredites to "gather together all the people upon all the face of the land, who had not been slain" (Ether 15:11-14).

[24] Mormon had given the plates to his son Moroni prior to the last great battle (Mormon 6:6). After that battle, Mormon recorded how his men had been hewn down (Mormon 6:10). He again had the plates. As Mormon put the small plates with his abridgment (Words of Mormon 1:5-6), he recorded, "I delivered these records into the hands of my son" (Words of Mormon 1:2). He had to be returning them.

[25] Joseph Smith did not record the size of the sealed portion of the Book of Mormon. There are four accounts concerning their size. Orson Pratt said that about two-thirds were sealed (*Journal of Discourses*, 3:347). On one occasion, David Whitmer stated that about half was sealed. At another time, he implied that two-thirds were sealed (Lyndon W. Cook, ed., *David Whitmer Interviews* (1991), 21, 75). George Q. Cannon wrote that about one-third was sealed (*A History of the Prophet Joseph Smith for Young People* (1957), 27). Which is correct?

The printer's manuscript of the Book of Mormon text was written on 464 pages of foolscap paper. Adding back the 116 pages of the lost manuscript sums up to 580 pages of foolscap. If the sealed portion were two-thirds of the plates, it would be about 1160 pages, one-half would be 580 pages, and one-third would be 290 pages. Mormon's portion of the Book of Mormon was on 422 pages of foolscap. If he copied the small plates of Nephi before attaching them to his plates, another 115 pages would be attributed to Mormon's hand for a total of 537 pages. His portion took about twenty-three years to complete. This means that Mormon wrote at a rate of eighteen to twenty-three pages per year. The sealed portion took as many as sixteen years to complete. If the sealed portion were two-thirds of the plates, Moroni would have written at a rate of over seventy-two pages per year, one-half would be thirty-six pages per year, and one-third would be eighteen pages per year. Where Mormon abridged and engraved, the sealed portion would have to be translated and engraved. It appears that abridging was more time consuming than translating. Most scholars give David

Whitmer's statements the most creditability, because he was one of the eleven witnesses who saw the plates.

George Q. Cannon wrote that all the plates were bound together on one edge by three rings, and that on the other edge, three smaller rings sealed the plates (*A History of the Prophet Joseph Smith for Young People* (1957), 27). David Whitmer was reported to have said that what was sealed appeared to be solid "as wood." There were "perceptible marks where the plates seemed to be sealed." The leaves of the sealed portion "were so securely bound together that it was impossible to separate them" (Lyndon W. Cook, ed., *David Whitmer Interviews* (1991), 20, 75, 221).

[26] Moroni began both the eighth chapter of Mormon and the Book of Moroni with an update of Lamanite affairs. This update is noticeably absent from the beginning of the Book of Ether. An update of Lamanite affairs would not have been necessary if only a short amount of time had elapsed between the writing of the last chapter of Mormon and the first chapter of Ether.

Another item noticeably absent from the Book of Ether is the date it was written. Moroni dated the eighth chapter of Mormon (Mormon 8:6) and the last chapter of the Book of Moroni (Moroni 10:1). Why had he not dated the Book of Ether? It is significant that the first verse of Ether starts with "And now I, Moroni, proceed to give an account of those ancient inhabitants…of this north country." Moroni did not begin the eighth chapter of Mormon or the Book of Moroni with an "And." With the simple statement of "And now I, Moroni, proceed to give an account" he effectively and efficiently connected the writing of the Book of Ether with the time of writing of the last two chapters of Mormon. After finishing his father's record, he immediately began abridging the Book of Ether. Moroni did not need to date the Book of Ether or update us on Lamanite affairs because he had already done so in the eighth chapter of Mormon, and only a short amount of time had elapsed.

Moroni began to write the eighth chapter of Mormon in 401. The question becomes when did he finish chapter nine of Mormon, the Book of Ether, and the title page of the Book of Mormon? This portion of the Book of Mormon was written on forty-one pages of foolscap paper. If the sealed portion of the plates were one-half to two-thirds of those plates, then Moroni translated at a rate of thirty-six to seventy-two pages of foolscap paper per year. This portion of the Book of Mormon could have been completed in the same year as it was started. This may explain why Moroni only mentioned dates twice. Only two dates were significant. In the above verse (Ether 1:1) Moroni mentioned the ancient inhabitants of *this* north country. This implies that Moroni was in the north country (the land northward) when the Book of Ether was abridged.

Moroni uses the word "farewell" only twice: first as he was writing of the last generation of the people of Jared (Ether 12:38), and the second in the final verse of the Book of Moroni. He began the Book of Moroni by explaining that "after having made an end of abridging the account of the people of Jared, I had supposed not to have written more, but I have not as yet perished." Moroni began his book with an explanation of his first farewell. Both farewells invite us to seek or come unto Christ that we might receive the grace of God. He made his intentions clear.

[27] A. Karl Larson and Katharine Miles Larson ed., *Diary of Charles Lowell Walker* (1980), 2:526; Orson F. Whitney, *Life of Heber C. Kimball* (1973), 436.

[28] H. Donl Peterson, *Moroni* (2000), 80.

[29] Mormon had reviewed other sacred records either prior to or as he was abridging Third Nephi (3 Nephi 5:9, 8:2, 19). Therefore Third Nephi was most likely written some time after Mormon had taken possession of all the sacred records. However there is another possible explanation. Mormon may have lived near the hill Shim during the time of the abridgment of Third Nephi, which would have given him access to the sacred records.

[30] In Mormon's abridgment of the forty-third chapter of Alma, there is a significant change of theme. He no longer included the great plan of salvation sermons of the time. Instead he focused on wars and military leaders. He stated simply, "We shall say no more concerning their preaching" (Alma 43:2).

It is significant that between 375 and 380, the focus of Mormon's life also changed from ministering the gospel to commanding the Nephite armies. Evidence suggests the latter part of the Book of Alma was abridged during this time. If Mormon abridged at a rate of eighteen pages (of foolscap) per year, the forty-third chapter of Alma would have been abridged in the middle of this time period. This suggests that the events of Mormon's life may have affected what he chose to abridge into the Book of Mormon.

[31] Fourth Nephi would be a definite candidate for this time period. It covers almost three centuries in four pages.

[32] Mormon's portion of the plates were completed between 362 and 385, a period of twenty-three years. Moroni's portion was completed

in about two years. Moroni began the last two chapters of Mormon and the Book of Ether in 401 and likely finished them that same year. The Book of Moroni was completed in 421. Because this portion was written on ten pages of foolscap, it was likely started and completed in the same year. This brings the total to twenty-five years. The years it took for Moroni to translate and write the sealed portion of the Book of Mormon were not added. The sealed portion was never meant to come forth with the Book of Mormon (Ether 4:6-7; 5:1). The title page of Book of Mormon makes no direct reference to it, which may indicate that the sealed portion of the Book of Mormon has its own title page.

[33] Mormon was born about 311. He began abridging the plates of Nephi in 362, and most likely completed his work in 385. During this period of time, he would have been between fifty-one and seventy-four years of age. My best guess is that Moroni was born about 350. He would have been about fifty-one when he added the last two chapters of Mormon and the Book of Ether to his father's work, and about seventy-one when he completed the Book of Moroni.

CHAPTER 2

Redemption

There is save one Messiah spoken of by the prophets, and that Messiah is he who should be rejected of the Jews. For according to the words of the prophets, the Messiah cometh in six hundred years from the time that my father left Jerusalem; and according to the words of the prophets, and also the word of an angel of God, his name shall be Jesus Christ, the Son of God. And now, by brethren, I have spoken plainly that ye cannot err.
(2 Nephi 25:18-20)

Elements of Redemption

The Book of Mormon is another testament of our Savior. Its core message is the testimony of prophets concerning Jesus Christ—that he is the Son of God, that he died and was buried, that he was resurrected and ascended into heaven, that he is the Redeemer of the world.

Nowhere in all of holy writ is the doctrine of redemption more fully revealed than in the Book of Mormon. With the publication of the Book of Mormon in 1830, this doctrine came forth without any fanfare. There were no celebrations. There were no evolutionary stages. It came forth as a fully developed doctrine with form and detail that still surprise and delight all who seek to come unto Christ.

Redemption is a major topic of the Book of Mormon. The word "redemption" is found fifty-one times in the Book of Mormon, and "redeem" and its inflected forms [redeemed, redeeming, redeemeth] are found another fifty-seven times, for a total of one hundred and eight entries; and that does not include the forty-one times that Jesus Christ is mentioned as the Redeemer. These entries reveal both the plan of redemption and the meaning of redemption.

The Book of Mormon charts the elements of redemption from the beginning to the end. As prophets of the Book of Mormon speak on redemption, they reveal other gifts and principles of the gospel of Jesus Christ that strengthen us as we attempt to walk in the strait and narrow path. These gifts and principles include:

- The agency of man.
- The plan of redemption.
- Being born of the Spirit.
- God's people.
- The presence of the Lord.
- Enduring to the end.

The Agency of Man

The Lord revealed to the Prophet Joseph Smith that "all truth is independent in that sphere in which God has placed it, *to act for itself*, as all intelligence also; otherwise there is no existence. Behold, here is the agency of man."[1] Book of Mormon prophets knew all about agency. Lehi taught that because of the redemption of Jesus Christ, the children of men "have become free forever, knowing good from evil; *to act for themselves*."[2] We frequently refer to the ability or freedom to choose good or evil as moral agency.

Agency is such a fundamental principle of the gospel of Jesus Christ that without it, righteousness could not be brought to pass, neither wickedness; our knowledge of good and evil would be inconsequential, because we could act on neither. Without agency the strait and narrow path could be laid out directly before us, but to no avail. The principle of agency is so fundamental that the Lord said that without it "there is no existence."[3]

The Plan of Redemption

God has only one plan for the redemption and salvation of his children, a plan mentioned twenty-nine times in the Book of Mormon. It is referred to as:

- The great and eternal plan of deliverance from death.[4]
- The great and eternal plan of redemption.[5]
- The great plan of happiness.[6]
- The great plan of mercy.[7]
- The great plan of redemption.[8]
- The great plan of salvation.[9]
- The great plan of the Eternal God.[10]
- The merciful plan of the great Creator.[11]
- The plan of happiness.[12]
- The plan of mercy.[13]
- The plan of our God.[14]
- The plan of redemption.[15]
- The plan of restoration [of the body to the soul].[16]
- The plan of salvation.[17]

God's plan is eternal, great, and merciful. Through Christ it "was prepared from the foundation of the world"[18] to bring forth happiness, mercy, redemption, salvation, deliverance from death, and the restoration [of the body to the soul].

Born of the Spirit

After being racked "with the pains of a damned soul" for three days and nights, Alma cried to the Lord Jesus Christ for mercy and his limbs received their strength.[19] He stood up and declared: "I have repented of my sins, and have been redeemed of the Lord; behold I am born of the Spirit."[20] He explained that "after wading through much tribulation, repenting nigh unto death, the Lord in mercy hath seen fit to snatch me out of an everlasting burning, and I am born of God. My soul hath been redeemed from the gall of bitterness and the bonds of iniquity."[21]

Alma had been born of the Spirit. He had repented of his sins and had received a remission of them. He had found peace.[22] He had been changed from his "carnal and fallen state" to a state of righteousness, and had become a new creature.[23] He had been filled with the Holy Ghost and tasted of the exceeding joy thereof.[24] He had beheld "the marvelous light of God." He had "been redeemed."[25]

God's People

The prophets of the Book of Mormon foretold that Christ would come to redeem his people.[26] God's people have a covenant relationship with him; they are "his covenant people."[27] The Lord will gather the house of Israel "from the four quarters of the earth," for they are the "ancient and long dispersed covenant people of the Lord."[28]

Jesus told the Nephites, "I will remember the covenant which I have made with my people; and I have covenanted with them that I would gather them together in mine own due time, that I would give unto them again the land of their fathers for their inheritance, which is the land of Jerusalem, which is the promised land unto them forever, saith the Father."[29]

As Alma was preaching repentance and faith on the Lord, there were those who desired to come into the fold of God and be called his people. After teaching them about serving one another and being witnesses of God at all times, Alma asked: "If this be the desire of your hearts, what have you against being baptized in the name of the Lord, as a witness before him that ye have entered into a covenant with him, that ye will serve him and keep his commandments, that he may pour out his Spirit more abundantly upon you?"[30] As we are baptized into Christ's church, we become numbered among his people, the house of Israel.[31] Through baptism we enter into a covenant with the Lord that we will serve him and keep his commandments throughout the remainder of our mortal lives.[32]

Making covenants with God presupposes that God has revealed to man that which is acceptable to him, that God has a prophet upon the earth. The Book of Mormon teaches us that there will be prophets among God's people.

The Presence of the Lord

The second and third chapters of Ether tell us of the great faith of the Jaredite people and their prophet, the brother of Jared. After being instructed of the Lord, the brother of Jared and his brethren built eight barges to cross the great sea. The prayer of the brother of Jared speaks volumes: "O Lord, I have performed the work which thou hast commanded me, and I have made the barges according as thou hast directed me. And behold, O Lord, in them there is no light; whither shall we steer? And also we shall perish, for in them we cannot breathe, save it is the air which is in them; therefore we shall perish."[33] The message is clear. The Jaredites had built eight barges according to the instructions of the Lord, without knowing how they would have light to steer or air to breathe; yet there is no indication that they ever murmured against the prophet of the Lord, or that Jared ever called his brother a fool for thinking he could build a ship and cross the great waters.[34]

The Lord answered the brother of Jared's prayer by instructing him only how to enhance the vessels to receive air to breathe.[35] The brother of Jared did as the Lord had commanded—he made the improvement to the vessels, that they might receive air. He then "cried again unto the Lord saying: O Lord, behold I have done even as thou has commanded me; and I have prepared the vessels for my people, and behold there is no light in them. Behold, O Lord, wilt thou suffer that we shall cross this great water in darkness?"[36]

The Lord answered his dutiful servant by explaining the difficulty of the problem, and asking:

> What will ye that I should do that ye may have light in your vessels? For behold, ye cannot have windows, for they will be dashed in pieces; neither shall ye take fire with you, for ye shall not go by the light of fire. For behold, ye shall be as a whale in the midst of the sea; for the mountain waves shall dash upon you. Nevertheless, I will bring you up again out of the depths of the sea; for the winds have gone forth out of my mouth, and also the rains and the floods have I sent forth. And behold, I prepare you against these things; for ye cannot cross this great deep save I prepare you against the waves of the sea, and

> the winds which have gone forth, and the floods which shall come. Therefore what will ye that I should prepare for you that ye may have light when ye are swallowed up in the depths of the sea?[37]

The record is silent on what trials the brother of Jared may have gone through as the Lord placed this burden on him. There was no mortal solution. The Lord's words "what will ye that I should prepare for you that ye may have light" must have resounded through his mind again and again.

The brother of Jared went to the mount Shelem, where he molten out of rock sixteen small, white, transparent stones, and carried them to the top of the mount.[38] He had done all he could do.

This would be the third time the brother of Jared approached the Lord in prayer in behalf of his people, that they might not have to cross the raging deep in darkness. He told the Lord of his weakness and unworthiness before him, then bore his solemn witness: "I know, O Lord, that thou hast all power, and can do whatsoever thou wilt for the benefit of man; therefore touch these stones, O Lord, with thy finger, and prepare them that they may shine forth in darkness."[39] Our text tells us, "The Lord stretched forth his hand and touched the stones one by one with his finger. And the veil was taken from off the eyes of the brother of Jared, and he saw the finger of the Lord."[40]

The brother of Jared fell to the earth, and the Lord asked, "Why hast thou fallen?"[41] He responded: "I saw the finger of the Lord."[42] When the Lord asked: "Sawest thou more than this?"[43] The brother of Jared answered: "Nay; Lord, show thyself unto me."[44] The Lord asked one final probing question: "Believest thou the words which I shall speak?"[45] The brother of Jared answered:

"Yea, Lord, I know that thou speakest the truth, for thou art a God of truth, and canst not lie."[46]

> And when he had said these words, behold, the Lord showed himself unto him, and said: Because thou knowest these things ye are redeemed from the fall; therefore ye are brought back into my presence; therefore I show myself unto you. Behold, I am he who was prepared from the foundation of the world to redeem my people. Behold, I am Jesus Christ. I am the Father and the Son. In me shall all mankind have life, and that eternally, even they who shall believe on my name; and they shall become my sons and my daughters.[47]

Because of the faith and knowledge of this man, he had been redeemed from the fall and brought back into the presence of the Lord.

Enduring to the End

Before Amaleki delivered the plates to king Benjamin, he exhorted "all men to come unto God," and to believe in the gifts that come from the Lord.[48] He then went on and listed the steps to salvation:

- I would that ye should *come* unto Christ, who is the Holy One of Israel,
- and *partake* of his salvation, and the power of his redemption.
- Yea, come unto him, and *offer* your whole souls as an offering unto him,
- and *continue* in fasting and prayer,
- and *endure* to the end;
- and as the Lord liveth ye will be saved.[49]

The message is clear. Even after partaking of the power of Christ's redemption, we must still endure to the end.

In his dream of the tree of life, Lehi saw those who would partake of the fruit of the tree, and later fall away:

> I beheld others pressing forward, and they came forth and caught hold of the end of the rod of iron; and they did press forward through the mist of darkness, clinging to the rod of iron, even until they did come forth and partake of the fruit of the tree. And after they had partaken of the fruit of the tree they did cast their eyes about as if they were ashamed. And I also cast my eyes round about, and beheld, on the other side of the river of water, a great and spacious building; and it stood as it were in the air, high above the earth. And it was filled with people, both old and young, both male and female; and their manner of dress was exceedingly fine; and they were in the attitude of mocking and pointing their fingers towards those who had come at and were partaking of the fruit. And after they had tasted of the fruit they were ashamed, because of those that were scoffing at them; and they fell away into forbidden paths and were lost.[50]

They had gone forth and partaken of the fruit of the tree of life, a fruit white even "to exceed all whiteness," which filled the "soul with exceeding great joy;" a fruit that was "most precious and most desirable" above all, "the greatest of all the gifts of God."[51] They had partaken of the power of Christ's redemption but had not continued in fasting and prayer, and had not endured to the end; thus they fell away and were lost.

As Nephi discussed the doctrine of Christ, he spoke of hearing the voice of the Son of God, saying: "After ye have repented of your sins, and witnessed unto the Father that ye are willing to keep my commandments, by the baptism of water, and have received the baptism of fire and of the Holy Ghost, and can speak with a new tongue, yea, even with the tongue of angels, and after this should deny me, it would have been better for you that ye had not known me."[52] Then Nephi heard the voice of the Father: "Yea, the words of my Beloved are true and faithful. He that endureth to the end, the same shall be saved."[53]

If the Father and the Son taught a prophet of Nephi's stature to endure to the end, then how much more need have we to be taught to endure to the end!

Notes

[1] D&C 93:30-31
[2] 2 Nephi 2:26; Alma 12:31; Helaman 14:30-31
[3] D&C 93:30
[4] 2 Nephi 11:5
[5] Alma 34:16
[6] Alma 42:8
[7] Alma 42:31
[8] Jacob 6:8; Alma 34:31
[9] Alma 42:5
[10] Alma 34:9
[11] 2 Nephi 9:6
[12] Alma 42:16
[13] Alma 42:15
[14] 2 Nephi 9:13
[15] Alma 12:25-26, 30, 32-33; 17:16; 18:39; 22:13; 29:2; 39:18; 42:11, 13
[16] Alma 41:2
[17] Jarom 1:2; Alma 24:14
[18] Alma 22:13
[19] Alma 36:16, 23; 38:8
[20] Mosiah 27:24
[21] Mosiah 27:28-29
[22] Alma 38:8
[23] Mosiah 27:25-26
[24] Alma 36:24
[25] Mosiah 27:29
[26] Mosiah 13:33; 18:20; Alma 5:21, 27; 6:8; 11:40; 33:22;Helaman 5:10; 3 Nephi 6:20; Ether 3:14
[27] 2 Nephi 6:17; 30:2
[28] 3 Nephi 16:5; Mormon 8:15
[29] 3 Nephi 20:29
[30] Mosiah 18:7-10
[31] 3 Nephi 21:6; 30:2
[32] Mosiah 18:10, 13
[33] Ether 2:18-19
[34] 1 Nephi 17:17
[35] Ether 2:18-19
[36] Ether 2:21-22
[37] Ether 2:23-25
[38] Ether 3:1
[39] Ether 3:2-4
[40] Ether 3:6
[41] Ether 3:6-7
[42] Ether 3:8
[43] Ether 3:9
[44] Ether 3:10
[45] Ether 3:11
[46] Ether 3:12
[47] Ether 3:13-14
[48] Omni 1:25
[49] Omni 1:26
[50] 1 Nephi 8:24-28
[51] 1 Nephi 8:11-12; 15:36
[52] 2 Nephi 31:14
[53] 2 Nephi 31:15

CHAPTER 3

The Plan of Redemption

How great the importance
to make these things known
unto the inhabitants of the earth.
(2 Nephi 2:8)

Components of the Plan

As Jarom began to write on the small plates of Nephi, he did not record his prophecies or revelations; instead he referred us to his fathers' writings on the plan of salvation:

> Now behold, I, Jarom, write a few words according to the commandment of my father, Enos, that our genealogy may be kept. And as these plates are small, and as these things are written for the intent of the benefit of our brethren the Lamanites, wherefore, it must needs be that I write a little; but I shall not write the things of my prophesying, nor of my revelations. For what could I write more than my fathers have written? For have not they revealed the plan of salvation? I say unto you, Yea; and this sufficeth me.[1]

His questions and answer leads one to ask: Where in the small plates did Jarom's fathers (Enos, Jacob, or Lehi) reveal the plan of salvation? How can we recognize these writings?

Four chapters in the Book of Mormon make multiple references to God's plan.[2] One would assume that these chapters might reveal a great deal about the plan of redemption, and they do. These sermons contain ten common components:

- Adam fell—man is fallen.[3]
- Life is a probationary state, a state to act.[4]
- There is a temporal and spiritual death.[5]
- Man may repent, have faith unto repentance.[6]
- God has given man commandments, his law.[7]
- God is both just and merciful.[8]
- The atonement of Jesus Christ is essential.[9]
- The dead will be resurrected.[10]
- There is a final judgment.[11]
- There is a final state.[12]

Anciently, a sermon on the plan of redemption contained specific elements. Knowledge of these elements suggests that Jarom was referring to the second and ninth chapters of Second Nephi when he stated that his fathers had "revealed the plan of salvation." The Book of Mormon contains other sermons about the plan of redemption. The words delivered to king Benjamin by an angel of the Lord[13] contain eight of the ten elements, and the words of the prophet Abinadi to king Noah and his priests[14] contain all ten components.

The Book of Mormon contains seven sermons on God's plan of salvation.[15] The message is clear. God wants us to know and understand this plan. Therefore he had it restored to the earth in 1830 with the publication of the Book of Mormon.

The Book of Mormon gives us numerous examples of individuals teaching the plan of redemption. Lehi taught it to his son Jacob.[16] Jacob taught it to the Nephites.[17] King Benjamin taught it to his people.[18] Abinadi taught it to king Noah and his priests.[19] Alma taught it to the people of the city of Ammonihah.[20] The sons of Mosiah taught it to the Lamanites.[21] Amulek taught it to the Zoramites.[22] Alma taught it to his son Corianton.[23]

Among the most powerful and unforgettable verses ever recorded by a prophet of God are those written by the hand of Alma:

> O that I were an angel, and could have the wish of mine heart, that I might go forth and speak with the trump of God, with a voice to shake the earth, and cry repentance unto every people! Yea, I would declare unto every soul, as with the voice of thunder, repentance and the plan of redemption, that they should repent and come unto our God, that there might not be more sorrow upon all the face of the earth.[24]

Alma knew that even the angels teach the plan of redemption.[25] The question now becomes: What did the prophets of ancient America teach about each of the components of the plan of redemption?

The Fall of Adam

If Adam had not transgressed he would have remained in the garden of Eden forever and had no end.[26] He would have remained in a state of innocence.[27] Some feel that if Adam had not fallen we would be better off, but Lehi taught that if Adam and Eve had not transgressed "they would have had no children."[28] Therefore, if Adam had not fallen we would not have been born, for "Adam fell that men might be."[29]

The fall of Adam brought upon man temporal and spiritual death. Temporal death is defined as "the death of the mortal body,"[30] and spiritual death as being "cut off from the presence of the Lord."[31]

Book of Mormon prophets saw the mortal state of being cut off from the presence of the Lord as a carnal, fallen, lost, or worthless state.[32] Man had fallen and "could not merit anything of himself."[33] Even if we should serve God with our whole souls, yet we "would be unprofitable servants."[34] For the law justified no flesh.[35] Therefore all mankind were fallen and in the grasp of the justice of God, "which consigned them forever to be cut off from his presence," except an atonement be made.[36]

A Probationary State

"After Adam and Eve had partaken of the forbidden fruit they were driven out of the garden of Eden, to till the earth." They brought forth children; "even the family of all the earth. And the days of the children of men were prolonged, according to the will of God, that they might repent while in the flesh; wherefore, their state became a state of probation."[37] This life became a "time for men to prepare to meet God," "a time to prepare for that endless state" which follows the resurrection.[38]

Having partaken of the tree of the knowledge of good and evil, Adam and Eve placed themselves "in a state to act according to their wills and pleasures, whether to do evil or do good." Therefore God gave unto men commandments, "that they should not do evil," the penalty thereof being "an everlasting death as to things pertaining unto righteousness."[39]

Book of Mormon prophets warn us again and again of the dangers of procrastinating or wasting the "day" of our repentance, for the man who will not repent "persists in his own carnal nature" and "remaineth in his fallen state."[40]

Death

"The first death" came upon mankind "by the fall of Adam."[41] It was both temporal and spiritual.[42] Temporal death is "the death of the mortal body."[43] Spiritual death is being "cut off from the presence of the Lord."[44] Jesus Christ "redeemeth all mankind from the first death."[45] Because of the atonement and resurrection of Christ, "this mortal shall put on immortality," and all are "brought back into the presence of the Lord" to be judged "according to their works."[46]

Men will not be punished for Adam's transgression, but for their own sins. Prophets of the Book of Mormon admonish us to repent. For there is a second death, which is "an everlasting death as to things pertaining unto righteousness," and "whosoever will harden his heart" and will do iniquity "shall not enter into the rest of the Lord."[47] The prophet Samuel warned that "whosoever repenteth not is hewn down and cast into the fire; and there cometh upon them again a spiritual death, yea, a second death, for they are cut off again as to things pertaining to righteousness. Therefore repent ye, repent ye, lest by knowing these things and not doing them ye shall suffer yourselves to come under condemnation, and ye are brought down unto this second death."[48]

Repentance

Knowing good from evil, men became free "to act for themselves," and time was granted unto man "to repent and serve God."[49] Book of Mormon prophets invite all to repent and come unto Christ.[50] Repentance is one of the first principles and ordinances that brings us to God, and should not be thought of as a burden. The prophet Moroni wrote, "if ye shall deny yourself of all ungodliness, and love God with all your might, mind and strength, then is his grace sufficient for you, that by his grace ye may be perfect in Christ."[51] This is repentance in its purest form. Repentance is not the burden. Sin is the burden. It deadens our spiritual senses. By turning away from sin we begin a wondrous journey from darkness into the light of Christ.

The Law

All the plan of redemption sermons contained in the Book of Mormon were given before the mortal ministry of Jesus Christ. Thus when "the commandments" and "the law" were mentioned in these sermons, the subject was the commandments and the law according to the law of Moses.[52]

Abinadi gave one of the best descriptions of the purpose of the law of Moses. He explained that because the children of Israel "were a stiffnecked people, quick to do iniquity, and slow to remember the Lord their God; therefore there was a law given them, yea, a law of performances and of ordinances, a law which they were to observe strictly from day to day, to keep them in remembrance of God and their duty towards him."[53] Nephi taught his people to keep the performances and ordinances of the law of Moses until Christ should rise from the dead and show himself unto the people; then "the words which he shall speak unto you shall be the law ye shall do."[54]

Months after his ascension into heaven, Christ manifested himself to those near the temple in the land Bountiful.[55] He taught:

> Think not that I am come to destroy the law or the prophets. I am not come to destroy but to fulfil; for verily I say unto you, one jot nor one tittle hath not passed away from the law, but in me it hath all been fulfilled. And behold, I have given you the law and the commandments of my Father, that ye shall believe in me, and that ye shall repent of your sins, and come unto me with a broken heart and a contrite spirit. Behold, ye have the commandments before you, and the law is fulfilled. Therefore come unto me and be ye saved; for verily I say unto you, that except ye shall keep my commandments, which I have commanded you at this time, ye shall in no case enter into the kingdom of heaven.[56]

Jesus, perceiving that some marveled and wondered concerning these teachings, further explained that "the law which was given unto Moses hath an end in me. Behold, I am the law, and the light. Look unto me, and endure to the end, and ye shall live; for unto him that endureth to the end will I give eternal life."[57]

Mormon confirmed that the people of Nephi "did not walk any more after the performances and ordinances of the law of Moses; but they did walk after the commandments which they had received from their Lord and their God, continuing in fasting and prayer, and in meeting together oft both to pray and to hear the word of the Lord."[58]

Book of Mormon prophets taught that where there was no law, there was no punishment. The blood of Jesus Christ atones for the sins of those who "die not knowing the will of God," or who sin ignorantly.[59] The law also has no power over little children. After inquiring of the Lord, the word of the Lord came to Mormon saying: "Listen to the words of Christ, your Redeemer, your Lord and your God. Behold, I came into the world not to call the righteous but sinners to repentance; the whole need no physician, but they that are sick; wherefore, little children are whole, for they are not capable of committing sin; wherefore the curse of Adam is taken from them in me, that it hath no power over them."[60] Therefore "little children are alive in Christ," as are those who "are without the law."[61]

Justice and Mercy

If God were not merciful, his justice would consign us "forever to be cut off from his presence."[62] For no flesh can dwell in the presence of God, "save it be though the merits, and mercy, and grace of the Holy Messiah."[63] But God is both just and merciful.[64] Therefore he found it expedient that there should be a great and last sacrifice. It is the atonement of the Jesus Christ that brings "about the bowels of mercy, which overpowereth justice, and bringeth means unto men that they may have faith unto repentance, ...while he that exercises no faith unto repentance is exposed to the whole law of the demands of justice; therefore only unto him that has faith unto repentance is brought about the great and eternal plan of redemption."[65]

The Atonement

"The whole meaning of the law of Moses" pointed to the "great and last sacrifice" of the Son of God. The intent of his sacrifice was "to bring about the bowels of mercy."[66] "There could have been no redemption for mankind" save it be "through the death and sufferings of

Christ, and the atonement of his blood."[67] For "all are hardened." "All are fallen" and lost, and must perish.[68] "Since man had fallen he could not merit anything of himself." It is "the sufferings and death of Christ" that "atone for our sins," through our "faith and repentance."[69]

The atonement of Jesus Christ is the very heart of the plan of redemption, bringing life to every part or portion of God's plan. Without the infinite atonement, which only the Son of God could make, the resurrection would not be brought to pass.[70] The prophet Jacob explained:

> It must needs be an infinite atonement—save it should be an infinite atonement this corruption could not put on incorruption. Wherefore, the first judgment which came upon man must needs have remained to an endless duration. And if so, this flesh must have laid down to rot and to crumble to its mother earth, to rise no more. O the wisdom of God, his mercy and grace! For behold, if the flesh should rise no more our spirits must become subject to that angel who fell from before the presence of the Eternal God, and become the devil, to rise no more. And our spirits must have become like unto him, and we become devils, angels to a devil, to be shut out from the presence of our God.[71]

Nothing short of an infinite atonement would "suffice for the sins of the world."[72] "How great the importance to make these things known unto the inhabitants of the earth."[73] It was "an angel from God" that made known to king Benjamin:

> Men drink damnation to their own souls except they humble themselves and become as little children, and believe that salvation was, and is, and is to come, in and through the atoning blood of Christ, the Lord Omnipotent. For the natural man is an enemy to God, and has been from the fall of Adam, and will be, forever and ever, unless he yields to the enticings of the Holy Spirit, and putteth off the natural man and becometh a saint through

> the atonement of Christ the Lord, and becometh as a child, submissive, meek, humble, patient, full of love, willing to submit to all things which the Lord seeth fit to inflict upon him, even as a child doth submit to his father.[74]

These are the views of one with an eternal prospective. Men of the world have taught and continue to teach that no atonement can be made for sins, but every man fares in this life according to his management; that every man prospers according to his genius, and conquers "according to his strength."[75] Each must choose which perspective to follow. Either we believe that Christ has atoned for our sins, or we do not.

The Resurrection

Prophets of the Book of Mormon foretold how the Savior would be crucified, and after he lay in a sepulchre for three days he would "rise from the dead."[76] As the Only Begotten of the Father, he has power to lay down his life and take it up again, "that he may bring to pass the resurrection of the dead, being the first that should rise."[77] Thus "the bands of death shall be broken, and the Son reigneth, and hath power over the dead; therefore, he bringeth to pass the resurrection of the dead."[78]

The resurrection "bringeth to pass a redemption from an endless sleep, from which sleep all men shall be awakened by the power of God when the trump shall sound; and they shall come forth, both small and great, and all shall stand before his [judgment] bar, being redeemed and loosed from this eternal band of death, which death is a temporal death."[79] Amulek taught that our "mortal body is raised to an immortal body, that is from death, even from the first death unto life, that they can die no more; their spirits uniting with their bodies, never to be divided; thus the whole becoming spiritual and immortal, that they can no more see corruption."[80]

The prophet Alma told his son: "The soul shall be restored to the body, and the body to the soul; yea, and every limb and joint shall be restored to its body; yea, even a hair of the head shall not be lost; but all things shall be restored to their proper and perfect frame."[81] Alma went on to instruct him:

> The meaning of the word restoration is to bring back again evil for evil, or carnal for carnal, or devilish for devilish—good for that which is good; righteous for that which is righteous; just for that which is just; merciful for that which is merciful. Therefore, my son, see that you are merciful unto your brethren; deal justly, judge righteously, and do good continually; and if ye do all these things then shall ye receive your reward; yea, ye shall have mercy restored unto you again; ye shall have justice restored unto you again; ye shall have a righteous judgment restored unto you again; and ye shall have good rewarded unto you again. For that which ye do send out shall return unto you again, and be restored.[82]

Even though "this mortal shall put on immortal, and this corruption shall put on incorruption;" yet we should not suppose that we "shall be restored from sin to happiness," or from wickedness to righteousness.[83] That will not happen.

Judgment

Prophets of the Book of Mormon foretold of meeting us before the pleasing bar of God, that "if they are condemned they bring upon themselves their own condemnation."[84] Alma explained:

> It is requisite with the justice of God that men should be judged according to their works; and if their works were good in this life, and the desires of their hearts were good, that they should also, at the last day, be restored unto that which is good. And if their works are evil they shall be restored unto them for evil. Therefore, all things shall be restored to their proper order, every thing to its natural frame—mortality raised to immortality, corruption to incorruption.... The one raised to happiness according to his desires of happiness, or good according to his desires of good; and the other to evil according to his desires of evil; for as he has desired to do evil all the day long even so shall he have his reward of evil when the night cometh. And so it is on the other hand. If he hath repented of his sins, and desired righteousness until the end of his days, even so he shall be rewarded unto righteousness. These are they that are redeemed of the Lord; yea, these are they that are taken out, that are delivered from that endless night of darkness; and thus they stand or fall; for behold, they are their own judges, whether to do good or do evil.[85]

As Mormon abridged his personal record, he explained one of his purposes of writing: "For this cause I write unto you, that ye may know that ye must all stand before the judgment-seat of Christ, yea, every soul who belongs to the whole human family of Adam; and ye must stand to be judged of your works, whether they be good or evil.... And I would that I could persuade all ye ends of the earth to repent and prepare to stand before the judgment-seat of Christ."[86]

The Final State

The Lord sent his angel to visit many of his people, declaring that "all men shall reap a reward of their works, according to that which they have been—if they have been righteous they shall reap the salvation of their souls, according to the power and deliverance of Jesus Christ; and if they have been evil they shall reap the damnation of their souls, according to the power and captivation of the devil."[87]

Those who do not repent "can in nowise inherit the kingdom of God."[88] Amulek explained to Zeezrom that "the Lord surely should come to redeem his people, but that he should not come to redeem them in their sins, but to redeem them from their sins. And he hath power given unto him from the Father to redeem them from their sins because of repentance."[89]

Prophets of the Book of Mormon taught that "no unclean thing can dwell with God."[90] Moroni explained that "ye would be more miserable to dwell with a holy and just God, under a consciousness of your filthiness before him, than ye would to dwell with the damned souls in hell."[91] Thus "the final state of the souls of men is to dwell in the kingdom of God, or to be cast out."[92]

God the Father loves all his children. He has provided a plan that gives each of us the agency and freedom to come unto Christ, our Savior and Redeemer, and become cleansed from all sin. Prophets of God continue to warn us to repent, that we may inherit the kingdom of God—anything less would be a form of damnation.

Notes

[1] Jarom 1:1-2
[2] 2 Nephi 9; Alma 12, 34, 42
[3] 2 Nephi 9:6; Alma 12:22; 34:9; 42:6, 9, 14
[4] 2 Nephi 9:27; Alma 12:24, 31; 34:31-33; 42:4, 10-13
[5] Nephi 9:10-12; Alma 12:23-24, 32; 42:6-9
[6] 2Nephi 9:23-24; Alma 12:24, 30, 32-34; 34:15-17, 30-35; 42:13, 16-18, 22-24
[7] 2 Nephi 9:23-27; Alma 12:31-32; 34:13-14; 42:16-23
[8] 2 Nephi 9:16-19; Alma 12:32-35; 34:15-18; 42:13-15, 21-25
[9] 2 Nephi 9:7, 25-26; Alma 34:8-12; 42:15, 22-23
[10] 2 Nephi 9:6, 11-14, 22; Alma 12:24-25; 42:22-23
[11] 2 Nephi 9:15, 22; Alma12:27; 42:22-23
[12] 2 Nephi 9:16-19; Alma 12:34-37; 34:35-36; 42:26
[13] Mosiah 3:3-27
[14] Mosiah 13:25-35; 15:1-31; 16:1-15
[15] 2 Nephi 2; 9; Mosiah 3; 13-16;Alma 12; 34; 42
[16] 2 Nephi 2
[17] 2 Nephi 9
[18] Mosiah 3
[19] Mosiah 13-16
[20] Alma 12
[21] Alma 17:16; 18:39; 22:13
[22] Alma 34
[23] Alma 42
[24] Alma 29:1-2
[25] Mosiah 3:1-27; Alma 12:29-30; 24:14; 39:18-19
[26] 2 Nephi 2:22
[27] 2 Nephi 2:23
[28] 2 Nephi 2:23
[29] 2 Nephi 2:25
[30] Alma 11:42, 45
[31] Alma 42:9
[32] 1 Nephi 10:6; Mosiah 4:5; 27:25
[33] Alma 22:14
[34] Mosiah 2:21
[35] 2 Nephi 2:5
[36] Alma 42:14-15
[37] 2 Nephi 2:19-21
[38] Alma 12:24; 34:32
[39] Alma 12:31-32
[40] 1 Nephi 10:20-21; 2 Nephi 9:27; Mosiah 16:5, 12; Alma 13:27; 34:33-36; Helaman 13:38
[41] Helaman 14:16
[42] Alma 11:45; Helaman 14:16
[43] Alma 11:42, 45
[44] Alma 42:9
[45] Helaman 14:16
[46] Mosiah 16:10; Alma 12:12; Helaman 14:17; Mormon 9:13-14
[47] Alma 12:32, 35-36
[48] Helaman 14:18-19
[49] 2 Nephi 2:26; Alma 42:4
[50] 1 Nephi 6:4; 10:18; 2 Nephi 9:45, 51; 26:25, 33; Jacob 1:7; Omni 1:26; 3 Nephi 9:22; Ether 4:18; 12:27
[51] Moroni 10:32
[52] 1 Nephi 4:15; 2 Nephi 5:10; Alma 34:13; Helaman 13:1; 15:5

[53] Mosiah 13:29-30
[54] 2 Nephi 25:30; 26:1; 32:6
[55] 3 Nephi 10:18-19; 11:1-10
[56] 3 Nephi 12:17-20
[57] 3 Nephi 15:2-9
[58] 4 Nephi 1:12
[59] 2 Nephi 9:26; Mosiah 3:11; 15:24-25; Moroni 8:22
[60] Moroni 8:7-8
[61] Moroni 8:22
[62] Alma 42:14
[63] 2 Nephi 2:8
[64] Alma 42:15
[65] Alma 34:14-16
[66] Alma 34:14-15
[67] Alma 21:9
[68] Alma 34:9
[69] Alma 22:14
[70] Alma 42:23
[71] 2 Nephi 9:7-9
[72] Alma 34:12
[73] 2 Nephi 2:8
[74] Mosiah 3:18-19
[75] Alma 30:17
[76] 2 Nephi 25:13
[77] 2 Nephi 2:8
[78] Mosiah 15:20
[79] Mormon 9:13
[80] Alma 11:45
[81] Alma 40:23
[82] Alma 41:13-15
[83] Mosiah 16:10; Alma 41:10-13; Mormon 9:14
[84] Jacob 6:13; Enos 1:27; Helaman 14:29; Moroni 10:34
[85] Alma 41:3-7
[86] Mormon 3:20, 22
[87] Alma 9:25, 28
[88] Alma 5:51; 9:12; 3 Nephi 11:38
[89] Helaman 5:10-11
[90] 1 Nephi 10:21; Alma 11:37; 3 Nephi 27:19
[91] Mormon 9:4
[92] 1 Nephi 15:35

CHAPTER 4

The Born-Again Experience

I have repented of my sins,
and have been redeemed of the Lord;
behold I am born of the Spirit.
(Mosiah 27:24)

Baptism of Fire and of the Holy Ghost

The Book of Mormon contains a number of expressions for "being born again," depending on who was teaching:

Nephi:	Baptism of fire and of the Holy Ghost.[1]
Benjamin:	Spiritually begotten, born of [Christ].[2]
Alma:	Born of the Spirit, born again, born of God.[3]
Aaron:	Born of God.[4]
Jesus Christ:	Baptize[d] with fire and with the Holy Ghost.[5]
Mormon:	Baptized with fire and with the Holy Ghost.[6]
Moroni:	Baptized with fire and with the Holy Ghost.[7]

Whether men and women were born again or baptized with fire and with the Holy Ghost, the results were the same. They were changed,[8] filled with the Holy Ghost,[9] received a remission of their sins,[10] praised God,[11] and taught others.[12]

The Meaning of Being Born Again

The term "born of the Spirit" suggests the beginning of a new life, a spiritual life. The born-again experiences recorded in the Book of Mormon are accounts of spiritual beginnings. Many were conversion experiences in which unbelievers began to believe, prayed, and received the Holy Spirit.

Some born-again experiences occurred to those who already believed, as when the twelve disciples of Christ were "filled with the Holy Ghost and with fire."[13] As the multitude witnessed the events of Christ's ministry, these events certainly marked the beginning of a spiritual revival, and probably identified the beginning of a new dispensation in ancient America.

Another example of a born-again experience among those who already believed occurred immediately after king Benjamin had spoken the words that had been delivered to him by an angel.[14] The Spirit of the Lord came upon the people, and they were "filled with joy" just as the angel had prophesied.[15] What was the spiritual root of this experience? It was both the prayer of king Benjamin and the prayer of the multitude.[16] This experience brought about a great remission of sins. King Benjamin could end his reign "with a clear conscience,"[17] and Mosiah would begin his reign with a kingdom that had been spiritually renewed.

The meaning of the born-again experience can be better understood by asking: What is the purpose of being born again? Nephi taught that "the gate by which ye should enter is repentance and baptism by water; then cometh a remission of your sins by fire and by the Holy Ghost. And then are ye in this strait and narrow path which leads to eternal life."[18] In other words, after you have received the baptism of fire and of the Holy Ghost, you are past the gate and "in this strait and narrow path which leads to eternal life." Through the atonement and mercy of Jesus Christ, you have received a remission of your sins and have received the Holy Ghost. You must now press forward along that path, "feasting upon the word of Christ."[19]

Moroni explained that "after they had been received unto baptism, and were wrought upon and cleansed by the power of the Holy Ghost, they were numbered among the people of the church of Christ; and their names were taken, that they might be remembered and nourished by the good word of God, to keep them in the right way, to keep them continually watchful unto prayer, relying alone upon the merits of Christ, who was the author and the finisher of their faith."[20] Notice that after they had been cleansed by the power of the Holy Ghost, they still were "nourished by the word of God, to keep them in the right way, to keep them continually watchful unto prayer, relying alone upon the merits of Christ." What fruit did they bring forth prior to baptism and being cleansed by the power of the Holy Ghost? It was "a broken heart and a contrite spirit;" they had "truly repented of all their sins."[21]

What works did Alma or Lamoni's father bring forth prior to being born again? They simply repented and called upon God. Their born-again experiences were testaments to the mercy of Christ, not to the works of men. The great works of these men came after they had been born again.

The Born Again Pattern

When the references to being born again are examined and compared, certain attributes stand out because of their repetition, they:

- believed the words of a servant of God,[22]
- had faith in Jesus Christ,[23]
- repented of their sins,[24]
- were baptized,[25]
- received the Spirit,[26]
- prayed unto the Lord,[27]
- received a remission of their sins,[28]
- found peace of conscience,[29]
- were changed,[30]
- became children of Christ, his sons and daughters,[31]
- praised God,[32]
- taught others.[33]

When these attributes are understood, other possible born-again experiences emerge: Lehi,[34] Nephi,[35] Enos,[36] Alma the elder,[37] Lamoni,[38] Mormon,[39] the twelve disciples of Christ,[40] and others who united with the church through baptism.[41] But if these were born-again experiences, why do these accounts not say so? The Lord informed those at Bountiful that when the three hundred Lamanites were baptized with fire and with the Holy Ghost, "they knew it not."[42] This may be a normal part of being born again; you simply know that you have received the Spirit. When king Benjamin's people were filled with joy, it was king Benjamin who announced to them, "This day [Christ] hath spiritually begotten you."[43]

Attributes of the Born Again Pattern

With each of the above attributes, the born-again experience is further defined and explained. By examining what Book of Mormon prophets taught concerning these attributes, a further understanding can be gained of what Alma meant when he said, "I have repented of my sins, and have been redeemed of the Lord; behold I am born of the Spirit."[44]

Believed the Word

The Prophet Joseph Smith taught that "faith comes by hearing the word of God, through the testimony of the servants of God; that testimony is always attended by the Spirit of prophecy and revelation."[45] The Book of Mormon gives example after example of individuals who heard the word of God before receiving the Spirit. Before Alma was born of the Spirit, he remembered his father's prophecy concerning Jesus Christ, who would come "to atone for the sins of the world."[46] Before Lamoni's father was born of God, Aaron had expounded the scriptures from the creation and the fall of man to "the sufferings and death of Christ."[47] Before the Spirit of the Lord came upon king Benjamin's people, they had heard their king speak "the words which had been delivered unto him by the angel of the Lord."[48] Mormon observed that "the preaching of the word had a great tendency to lead the people to do that which was just—yea, it had had more powerful effect upon the minds of the people than the sword, or anything else, which had happened unto them."[49]

Faith in Jesus Christ

As Moroni was completing the Book of Ether, his tone became discouraged: "Ether did prophesy great and marvelous things unto the people, which they did not believe, because they saw them not."[50] Moroni had already recorded "the sad tale of the destruction of [his] people."[51] He now faced an equally sad task of recording the annihilation of the once great Jaredite nation. He knew only too well the consequences of unbelief. He therefore spoke of the remedy: "I would show unto the world that faith is things which are hoped for and not seen; wherefore, dispute not because ye see not, for ye receive no witness until after the trial of your faith."[52] He noted that the miracle of change among the Lamanites was wrought by faith.[53] Mormon recorded that the Spirit of the Lord came upon the people of king Benjamin "because of the exceeding faith which they had in Jesus Christ."[54]

Repentance

Repentance brings forgiveness. The Lord and his saints will forgive those who turn away from their sins and seek first the kingdom of God and His righteousness. Alma and the sons of Mosiah are examples to all who seek to repent and serve God. They considered themselves among the greatest of all sinners and felt that they must do everything possible to make up for what they had done. No price was too great. The sons of Mosiah were willing to risk their lives to teach the gospel to the Lamanites, even before the Lord promised Mosiah that he would deliver his "sons out of the hands of the Lamanites."[55] His sons had not only changed, "they were desirous that salvation should be declared to every creature, for they could not bear that any human soul should perish; yea, even the very thoughts that any soul should endure endless torment did cause them to quake and tremble. And thus did the Spirit of the Lord work upon them."[56] These were the fruits that repentance had wrought into their lives.

Baptism

The Savior was baptized to fulfill all righteousness, thereby showing "unto the children of men that, according to the flesh he humbleth himself before the Father, and witnesseth unto the Father that he would be obedient unto him in keeping his commandments."[57] If we wish to follow the Savior we must also "witness unto the Father" though baptism that we are willing to take upon us "the name of Christ" and keep his commandments.[58] "The first fruits of repentance is baptism."[59] Alma asked: "What have you against being baptized in the name of the Lord, as a witness before him that ye have entered into a covenant with him, that ye will serve him and keep his commandments, that he may pour out his Spirit more abundantly upon you?"[60] Our baptism is a witness and a testimony before God that we are willing to serve him and keep his commandments.[61]

Received the Spirit

The fruits of being born again are joy and peace.[62] Some of those who were born again experienced the gift of prophecy.[63] This should not be surprising. Joseph Smith explained that the spirit of prophecy is the testimony of Jesus.[64] In other words, the testimony of Jesus comes through the spirit of prophecy. Mormon noted that the Spirit of the Lord came upon king Benjamin's people "because of the exceeding faith which they had in Jesus Christ."[65] The spirit of prophecy and the testimony of Jesus are the fruits of such "exceeding faith." "These gifts come by the Spirit of Christ," for "every good gift comes of Christ."[66] He is "the fountain of all righteousness."[67]

Prayer

The Spirit is received through prayer.[68] Before the Spirit of the Lord came upon king Benjamin's people, they cried: "O have mercy, and apply the atoning blood of Christ that we may receive forgiveness of our sins, and our hearts may be purified."[69] Before Alma was born again, he cried: "O Jesus, thou Son of God, have mercy on me, who am in the gall of bitterness, and am encircled about by the everlasting chains of death."[70] Before Lamoni's father was born of God, he cried: "O God, Aaron hath told me that there is a God; and if there is a God, and if thou art God, wilt thou make thyself known unto me, and I will give away all my sins to know thee."[71] Before the Holy Spirit of God came down from heaven and entered into the hearts of the three hundred Lamanites and filled them as if with fire, they cried unto the voice who had shaken the earth "until the cloud of darkness was dispersed."[72] Before the twelve disciples were filled with the Holy Ghost and with fire, they prayed for that which they most desired, "that the Holy Ghost should be given unto them."[73]

Remission of Sins

The first principles and ordinances of the gospel are given to us that we might receive a remission of our sins, grow in the knowledge and glory of God, bring forth works of righteousness, and enter into His kingdom. A remission of sins is received through prayer,[74] faith in Christ,[75] repentance,[76] baptism,[77] and receiving the Holy Ghost.[78] A remission of sins is retained by always remembering the goodness and long-suffering of God, remaining humble, calling on the Lord daily, standing steadfastly in the faith which is in Christ, and imparting of our substance to the poor.[79] It is the merciful who shall obtain mercy.[80] The Prophet Joseph Smith taught that "the nearer we get to our heavenly Father, the more we are disposed to look with compassion on perishing souls; we feel that we want to take them upon our shoulders, and cast their sins behind our backs.... If you would have God have mercy on you, have mercy on one another."[81]

Peace of Conscience

Nephi taught his people to look to Christ "for a remission of their sins."[82] It was because of the "exceeding faith" which king Benjamin's people had in Jesus Christ that the Spirit of the Lord came upon them, and they were filled with joy, having received a remission of their sins, and they had "peace of conscience."[83] After three hundred Lamanites were baptized with fire and with the Holy Ghost, there came a voice unto them saying: "Peace, peace be unto you because of your faith in my Well Beloved."[84] Alma related to his son that he was "three days and three nights in the most bitter pain and anguish of soul; and never, until I did cry out unto the Lord Jesus Christ for mercy, did I receive a remission of my sins. But behold, I did cry unto him and I did find peace to my soul."[85] Enos recorded that after he received a remission of his sins, his guilt was swept away. When he asked how it was done, he was told: "Because of thy faith in Christ."[86]

A Mighty Change

King Benjamin's people declared that the Spirit of the Lord "wrought a mighty change in us, or in our hearts, that we have no more disposition to do evil, but to do good continually."[87] As Alma was born again, the Lord said unto him: "Marvel not that all mankind, yea, men and women, all nations, kindreds, tongues and people, must be born again; yea, born of God, changed from their carnal and fallen state, to a state of righteousness, being redeemed of God."[88] Mormon taught his people, "That which is of God inviteth and enticeth to do good continually.... All things which are good cometh of Christ; otherwise men were fallen, and there could no good thing come unto them."[89] It is the Spirit of the Lord that "persuadeth men to do good."[90]

His Sons and His Daughters

It is the Spirit of the Lord that brings about the mighty change. Our hearts are changed through faith on Christ's name, and we are born of him and "become his sons and his daughters."[91] We become new creatures, changed from our "carnal and fallen state" to a state of righteousness, "becoming his sons and daughters."[92] Mormon taught: "If ye will lay hold upon every good thing, and condemn it not, ye certainly will be a child of Christ."[93] As we receive him, we become "the sons [and daughters] of God."[94]

Praised God

When the Spirit of the Lord came upon king Benjamin's people, they knew it was "through the infinite goodness of God," and they did "rejoice."[95] Nephi taught his people that after they received the Holy Ghost, "then can ye speak with the tongue of angels, and shout praises unto the Holy One of Israel."[96] Alma asked those at Zarahemla: "If ye have experienced a change of heart, and if ye have felt to sing the song of redeeming love, I would ask, can ye feel so now?"[97] Alma related his born-again experience by quoting Lehi when he thought he "saw God sitting upon his throne, surrounded with numberless concourses of angels in the attitude of singing and praising their God;" and Alma continued: "and my soul did long to be there."[98]

Taught Others

Alma explained to his son that from the time he was born of God, "I have labored without ceasing, that I might bring souls unto repentance."[99] The sons of Mosiah also zealously strove "to repair all the injuries which they had done to the church, confessing all their sins, and publishing all the things which they had seen, and explaining the prophecies and the scriptures to all who desired to hear them."[100] After Lamoni's father was born of God, he administered unto the multitude that had gathered.[101] After the three hundred Lamanites were baptized with fire and with the Holy Ghost, "they did go forth, and did minister unto the people, declaring throughout all the regions round about all things which they had heard and seen, insomuch that the more part of the Lamanites were convinced of them, because of the greatness of the evidences which they had received."[102]

Notes

[1] 2 Nephi 31:13, 14, 17
[2] Mosiah 5:7
[3] Mosiah 27:24, 25, 28; Alma 5:14, 49; 7:14; 36:5, 23, 24, 26; 38:6
[4] Alma 22:15
[5] 3 Nephi 9:20; 11:35; 12:1
[6] Mormon 7:10
[7] Ether 12:14
[8] Mosiah 5:7; 27:25; Ether 12:14
[9] Alma 36:24; 3 Nephi 19:13
[10] 2 Nephi 31:17; Alma 38:8
[11] 2 Nephi 31:13; Alma 5:26; 36:22, 28
[12] Mosiah 27:32; Alma 22:23; 36:24; Helaman 5:50
[13] 3 Nephi 19:13
[14] Mosiah 4:1
[15] Mosiah 3:4; 4:3
[16] Mosiah 3:4; 4:2
[17] Mosiah 2:15, 27
[18] 2 Nephi 31:17-18
[19] 2 Nephi 31:20
[20] Moroni 6:4
[21] Moroni 6:2
[22] Mosiah 4:3; 5:2, 4; Alma 22:15; 36:17-18; 3 Nephi 11:35; 12:1-2
[23] Mosiah 4:3; 5:7; Alma 7:14; Helaman 5:41
[24] 2 Nephi 31:13, 17; Mosiah 4:10; 27:24, 28; Alma 7:14; 22:18; 3 Nephi 11:35-38
[25] 2 Nephi 31:13, 17; Alma 7:14; 3 Nephi 11:33-38; 12:1-2; Mormon 7:10
[26] 2 Nephi 31:13; Mosiah 4:3, 12, 20; Alma 36:20, 24; Helaman 5:44
[27] Mosiah 4:2; Alma 22:17-18; 36:18; 38:8; Helaman 5:42
[28] Mosiah 4:3, 11; Alma 7:14; 38:8; 3 Nephi 12:2
[29] Mosiah 4:3; Alma 38:8; Helaman 5:47
[30] Mosiah 5:2; 27:25; Alma 5:14, 26
[31] Mosiah 5:7; 27:25
[32] 2 Nephi 31:13; Alma 5:26
[33] Mosiah 27:32; Alma 22:23-24; 36:23, Helaman 5:50
[34] 1 Nephi 1:4-18
[35] 1 Nephi 2:16-18
[36] Enos 1:1-19
[37] Mosiah 18:7-22
[38] Alma 18:23-43; 19:1-36
[39] Mormon 1:15-16
[40] 3 Nephi 19:9-15
[41] 3 Nephi 26:17-19; 28:18; 4 Nephi 1:1, Moroni 6:2-4
[42] 3 Nephi 9:20
[43] Mosiah 5:7
[44] Mosiah 27:24
[45] *Teachings of the Prophet Joseph Smith* (1976), 148.
[46] Alma 36:17
[47] Alma 22:13-14
[48] Mosiah 4:1
[49] Alma 31:5
[50] Ether 12:5
[51] Mormon 8:3
[52] Ether 12:6
[53] Ether 12:14-15
[54] Mosiah 4:3

[55] Mosiah 28:1-7; Alma 17:35; 19:23
[56] Mosiah 28:3-4
[57] 2 Nephi 31:6-7
[58] 2 Nephi 31:13-14
[59] Moroni 8:25
[60] Mosiah 18:10
[61] Mosiah 18:10; 21:35; 3 Nephi 7:25
[62] Mosiah 4:3; Alma 36:20-21; 38:8; Helaman 5:44, 47
[63] Mosiah 5:3; 27:30
[64] *Teachings of the Prophet Joseph Smith* (1976), 269.
[65] Mosiah 4:3
[66] Moroni 10:17-18
[67] Ether 12:28
[68] D&C 42:14; 63:64
[69] Mosiah 4:2-3
[70] Alma 36:18
[71] Alma 22:18
[72] Helaman 5:42-45
[73] 3 Nephi 19:9-13
[74] Enos 1:2-5; Mosiah 4:2-3, 20; Alma 38:8; Moroni 8:26
[75] Enos 1:2-8; 3 Nephi 7:16; Moroni 8:25
[76] Alma 12:34; Helaman 14:13; 3 Nephi 1:23; 7:16, 25; Moroni 8:11
[77] 3 Nephi 1:23; 12:2; 30:2; Moroni 8:11, 25
[78] 2 Nephi 31:17; Mosiah 4:3, 20; 3 Nephi 12:2; Moroni 8:26
[79] Mosiah 4:11-12, 26; Alma 4:13-14
[80] 3 Nephi 12:7
[81] *Teachings of the Prophet Joseph Smith* (1976), 241.
[82] 2 Nephi 25:26
[83] Mosiah 4:3
[84] Helaman 5:45-47; 3 Nephi 9:20
[85] Alma 38:8
[86] Enos 1:2-8
[87] Mosiah 5:2
[88] Mosiah 27:25
[89] Moroni 7:13, 24
[90] Ether 4:11
[91] Mosiah 5:7; Ether 3:14
[92] Mosiah 27:25-26
[93] Moroni 7:19
[94] D&C 11:30
[95] Mosiah 5:3-4
[96] 2 Nephi 31:13
[97] Alma 5:26
[98] 1 Nephi 1:8; Alma 36:22
[99] Alma 36:23-24
[100] Mosiah 27:35
[101] Alma 22:24-25
[102] Helaman 5:50

CHAPTER 5

The Presence of the Lord

Because thou knowest these things
ye are redeemed from the fall;
therefore ye are brought back into my presence;
therefore I show myself unto you.
(Ether 3:13)

Who Could Not Be Kept from Within the Veil

Moroni noted that "there were many whose faith was so exceedingly strong, even before Christ came, who could not be kept from within the veil, but truly saw with their eyes the things which they had beheld with an eye of faith, and they were glad. And behold, we have seen that one of these was the brother of Jared."[1] Although we are left to wonder who the "many" were, one thing seems certain—Nephi was most likely one of them. There are seven parallels between the brother of Jared's experience and Nephi's vision of the tree of life:

- Both took place on exceedingly high mountains.[2]
- Both received according to their desires.[3]
- Both were tested.[4]
- Both became witnesses of Jesus Christ.[5]
- Both were shown things which were not to go forth unto the world.[6]

- Both were given visions of things, which had been and would be, even unto the end of the world.[7]
- Both had been in the presence of the Lord.[8]

As we study the parallels between these two visions, it becomes more and more apparent that the experiences of Nephi and the brother of Jared were extremely similar.

Exceedingly High Mountains

Moroni recorded that "the brother of Jared, went forth unto the mount, which they called mount Shelem, because of its exceeding height, ...and cried again unto the Lord."[9]

Nephi wrote: "As I sat pondering in mine heart I was caught away in the Spirit of the Lord, yea, into an exceedingly high mountain, which I never had before seen, and upon which I never had before set my foot."[10] Nephi later noted: "And I, Nephi, did go into the mount oft, and I did pray oft unto the Lord; wherefore the Lord showed unto me great things."[11] Although there may have been others, the Book of Mormon records only the experiences of Nephi and the brother of Jared upon exceedingly high mountains.

Desire

The brother of Jared "did molten out of a rock sixteen small stones; and they were white and clear, even as transparent glass; and he did carry them in his hands upon the top of the mount" and cried unto the Lord: "O Lord, thou hast given us a commandment that we must call upon thee, that from thee we may receive according to our desires."[12] He continued: "Therefore touch these stones, O Lord, with thy finger, and prepare them that they may shine forth in darkness; and they shall shine forth unto us in the vessels which we have prepared, that we may have light while we shall cross the sea."[13] As the Lord touched the stones one by one with his finger, "the veil was taken from off the eyes of the brother of Jared, and he saw the finger of the Lord."[14] The brother of Jared fell to the earth, and the Lord asked, "Why hast thou fallen?"[15] He responded: "I saw the finger of the Lord."[16] When the Lord asked, "Sawest thou more than this?"[17] the brother of Jared answered, "Nay; Lord show thyself unto me."[18] He had a new desire.

After Nephi had been carried away upon an exceedingly high mountain, by the Spirit of the Lord, the Spirit said unto him: "Behold, what desirest thou?"[19] He responded: "I desire to behold the things which my father saw."[20]

A Final Test

As Moroni was concluding his father's writings, he recorded a promise unto all, even unto the ends of the earth: "Whoso believeth in Christ, doubting nothing, whatsoever he shall ask the Father in the name of Christ it shall be granted him."[21] Then seeming to sense that some of his readers might miss the importance of these words, he revealed that Jesus Christ had taught his disciples: "Whosoever shall believe in my name, doubting nothing, unto him will I confirm all my words, even unto the ends of the earth."[22]

Belief in Christ bears fruits. The knowledge of the brother of Jared became such that "he could not be kept from beholding within the veil; and he saw the finger of Jesus, which, when he saw, he fell with fear; for he knew that it was the finger of the Lord; and he had faith no longer, for he knew, nothing doubting."[23] Yet even after this, there was still one last test. When the brother of Jared requested: "Lord, show thyself unto me," the Lord responded: "Believest thou the words which I shall speak?"[24] He answered: "Yea, Lord, I know that thou speakest the truth, for thou art a God of truth, and canst not lie."[25] It is significant that his final test was one of belief, which assessed both his faith in God and his knowledge of the character of God.

After Nephi had done the things that the Lord had commanded him,[26] as he desired to behold the things that his father had seen, the Spirit queried: "Believest thou that thy father saw the tree of which he hath spoken?"[27] Nephi responded: "Yea, thou knowest that I believe all the words of my father."[28] The tests of the brother of Jared and Nephi could be considered the same, for the Lord made known through the Prophet Joseph Smith that "whether by mine own voice or by the voice of my servants, it is the same."[29] To believe the words of the prophet of the Lord is to believe the word of the Lord.

Witnesses of Christ

After the brother of Jared had said, "Yea, Lord, I know that thou speakest the truth, for thou art a God of truth, and canst not lie," the Lord showed himself unto him, and said: "Because thou knowest these things ye are redeemed from the fall; therefore ye are brought back into my presence; therefore I show myself unto you. Behold,

I am he who was prepared from the foundation of the world to redeem my people. Behold, I am Jesus Christ."[30]

After Nephi had said, "Yea, thou knowest that I believe all the words of my father," he witnessed the ministry of the Son of God.[31] He saw the Lamb of God going forth "ministering unto the people, in power and great glory."[32] He beheld that he would be "judged of the world" and "lifted up upon the cross and slain for the sins of the world."[33] Nephi later declared: "My soul delighteth to prophesy concerning him, for I have seen his day."[34]

Shown Things Not To Go Forth Unto the World

Having a perfect knowledge of God, the brother of Jared could not be kept from within the veil; "therefore he saw Jesus; and he did minister unto him. And it came to pass that the Lord said unto the brother of Jared: Behold, thou shalt not suffer these things which ye have seen and heard to go forth unto the world, until the time cometh that I shall glorify my name in the flesh; wherefore, ye shall treasure up the things which ye have seen and heard, and show it to no man."[35]

After Nephi had witnessed the Son of God, the fall of his people, and the restoration of the gospel among the Gentiles, he was told by the angel: "The things which thou shalt see hereafter thou shalt not write; for the Lord God hath ordained the apostle of the Lamb of God that he should write them. And also others who have been, to them hath he shown all things, and they have written them; and they are sealed up to come forth in their purity, according to the truth which is in the Lamb, in the own due time of the Lord."[36] Later he reminisced: "Mine eyes have beheld great things, yea, even too great for man; therefore I was bidden that I should not write them."[37]

Shown Things Past and Present

Moroni recorded that the Lord "showed unto the brother of Jared all the inhabitants of the earth which had been, and also all that would be; and he withheld them not from his sight, even unto the ends of the earth."[38] Moroni later wrote that "after the brother of Jared had beheld the finger of the Lord, because of the promise which the brother of Jared had obtained by faith, the Lord could not withhold anything from his sight; wherefore he showed him all things, for he could no longer be kept without the veil."[39]

Nephi wrote that "the angel spake unto me, saying: Look! And I looked and beheld a man, and he was dressed in a white robe. And the angel said unto me: Behold one of the twelve apostles of the Lamb. Behold, he shall see and write the remainder of these things; yea, and also many things which have been. And he shall also write concerning the end of the world. ...And behold, the things which this apostle of the Lamb shall write are many things which thou hast seen; and behold, the remainder shalt thou see. ...And I, Nephi heard and bear record, that the name of the apostle of the Lamb was John, according to the word of the angel."[40]

The Presence of the Lord

Moroni recorded that "the Lord commanded the brother of Jared to go down out of the mount from the presence of the Lord, and write the things which he had seen."[41] Jesus had "showed himself unto this man in the spirit" and had "ministered unto him even as he [had] ministered unto the Nephites; and all this, that this man might know that he was God, because of the many great works which the Lord had showed unto him."[42]

As Nephi spoke of the death and resurrection of the Messiah, he said that the wicked among his people should perish.[43] He continued: "O the pain, and the anguish of my soul for the loss of the slain of my people! For I, Nephi, have seen it, and it well nigh consumeth me before the presence of the Lord."[44] Nephi would have seen this destruction among his people during his vision of the tree of life.[45]

In Conclusion

The parallels between the visions of Nephi and the brother of Jared are noteworthy. Through the Book of Ether, Moroni gave us a second witness to many of the things Nephi had experienced. Moroni did not want us to see these experiences as exclusive, for he noted: "There were many whose faith was so exceedingly strong, even before Christ came, who could not be kept from within the veil."[46] His message is clear—through faith in Jesus Christ we may be redeemed from the fall and brought back into the presence of the Lord. But perhaps even most comforting to us individually is his second witness that the Lord is ever mindful of the desires and prayers of those who serve him.

Notes

[1] Ether 12:19-20
[2] 1 Nephi 11:1; Ether 3:1
[3] 1 Nephi 11:2, 6; Ether 3:2, 10
[4] 1 Nephi 11:4-5; Ether 3:11-12
[5] 1 Nephi 11:7; Ether 3:14
[6] 1 Nephi 14:28; Ether 3:21
[7] 1 Nephi 14:18-22, 24: Ether 3:25
[8] 2 Nephi 26:7; Ether 3:13; 4:1
[9] Ether 3:1
[10] 1 Nephi 11:1
[11] 1 Nephi 18:3
[12] Ether 3:1-2
[13] Ether 3: 4
[14] Ether 3:6
[15] Ether 3:6-7
[16] Ether 3:8
[17] Ether 3:9
[18] Ether 3:10
[19] 1 Nephi 11:1-2
[20] 1 Nephi 11:3
[21] Mormon 9:21
[22] Mormon 9:25
[23] Ether 3:19
[24] Ether 3:10-11
[25] Ether 3:12
[26] 1 Nephi 3:5-7; 4:38; 7:1-2, 22
[27] 1 Nephi 11:3-4
[28] 1 Nephi 11:5
[29] D&C 1:38
[30] Ether 3:12-14
[31] 1 Nephi 11:5-7, 20-21, 24
[32] 1 Nephi 11:27-28
[33] 1 Nephi 11:31-33
[34] 2 Nephi 25:13
[35] Ether 3:20-21
[36] 1 Nephi 14:25-26
[37] 2 Nephi 4:25
[38] Ether 3:25
[39] Ether 12:21
[40] 1 Nephi 14:18-22, 24, 27
[41] Ether 4:1
[42] Ether 3:17-18
[43] 2 Nephi 26:3
[44] 2 Nephi 26:7
[45] 1 Nephi 12:1-5
[46] Ether 12:19

A Chronology of the Book of Mormon

To every thing there is a season,
and a time to every purpose under the heaven.
(Ecclesiastes 3:1)

Small Plates of Nephi

600 B.C. (1 Nephi 2:4)[1]
[Lehi] departed into the wilderness
592 (1 Nephi 17:4)[2]
for the space of many years, yea, even eight years
570 (2 Nephi 5:28)[3]
thirty years had passed away from the time we left Jerusalem
560 (2 Nephi 5:34)
forty years had passed away
545 (Jacob 1:1)
fifty and five years had passed away from the time that Lehi left Jerusalem
421 (Enos 1:25)
an hundred and seventy and nine years had passed away from the time that our father Lehi left Jerusalem
400 (Jarom 1:5)
two hundred years had passed away
362 (Jarom 1:13)
two hundred and thirty and eight years had passed away

324 B.C. (Omni 1:3)
two hundred and seventy and six years had passed away
318 (Omni 1:3)
two hundred and eighty and two years had passed away
280 (Omni 1:5)
three hundred and twenty years had passed away

Words of Mormon

About 160-155 (Words of Mormon 1:10, 12-18)[4]
after Amaleki had delivered up these plates into the hands of king Benjamin (10)
the prophets, did once more establish peace in the land (18)

Book of Mosiah [5]

About 155 B.C. (Mosiah 1:1)
king Benjamin had continual peace all the remainder of his days
154-124 (Mosiah 1:2-9)[6]
[king Benjamin] had three sons; and he called their names Mosiah, and Helorum, and Helaman (2)
124 (Mosiah 1:10-6:4)[7]
making in the whole, about four hundred and seventy-six years from the time that Lehi left Jerusalem (6:4)
124-121 (Mosiah 6:5-7)
king Benjamin lived three years and he died (5)
for the space of three years (7)
121 (Mosiah 7:1-8:21; 25:1-18)
after…the space of three years (7:1)
121-About 100 (Mosiah 25:19-24)
About 100-91 (Mosiah 26:1-28:8)
there were many…being little children at the time [king Benjamin] spake unto his people (26:1)
91 (Mosiah 28:9-29:47)[8]
[sons of Mosiah] took their journey into the wilderness (28:9)
thus commenced the reign of the judges (29:44)
five hundred and nine years from the time Lehi left Jerusalem (29:46)

The Record of Zeniff

About 200-121 (Mosiah 9-22)

An Account of Alma

About 145-121 (Mosiah 23-24)[9]

Book of Alma

91 B.C. (Alma 1:1-21)[10]
in the first year of the reign of the judges (1)
in the first year of the reign of Alma in the judgment-seat (2)
90-88 (Alma 1:22-33)
in the second year of the reign of Alma (23)
until the fifth year of the reign of the judges (33)
87 (Alma 2:1-3:27)
in the commencement of the fifth year of their reign (2:1)
were commenced and ended in the fifth year of the reign of the judges (3:25)
thus endeth the fifth year of the reign of the judges (3:27)
86 (Alma 4:1-4)
in the sixth year of the reign of the judges (1)
85 (Alma 4:5)
in the seventh year of the reign of the judges
thus ended the seventh year of the reign of the judges
84 (Alma 4:6-10)
in the eighth year of the reign of the judges (6)
in this eighth year of the reign of the judges (9)
thus ended the eighth year of the reign of the judges (10)
83 (Alma 4:11-8:2)
in the commencement of the ninth year (4:11)
thus in the commencement of the ninth year of the reign of the judges (4:20)
thus ended the ninth year of the reign of the judges (8:2)
82 (Alma 8:3-15:19)
in the commencement of the tenth year of the reign of the judges (8:3)
even until the fourth day of this seventh month, which was is in the tenth year (10:6)

on the twelfth day, in the tenth month, in the tenth year of the reign of the judges (14:23)
thus ended the tenth year of the reign of the judges (15:19)
81 B.C. (Alma 16:1-11)
in the eleventh year of the reign of the judges...on the fifth day of the second month (1)
even until the fifth day of the second month in the eleventh year (1)
thus ended the eleventh year of the judges (9)
81-78 (Alma 16:12-21)
until the fourteenth year of the reign of the judges (12)
thus for three years (12)
thus ended the fourteenth year of the reign of the judges (21)
77 (Alma 17:1-4; 27:16-28:9)
thus endeth the fifteenth year of the reign of the judges (28:7)
the fifteenth year of the reign of the judges is ended (28:9)
76 (Alma 29:1-30:4)
in the sixteenth year of the reign of the judges (30:2)
in all the sixteenth year of the reign of the judges (30:4)
75 (Alma 30:5-35:12)
in the commencement of the seventeenth year of the reign of the judges (30:5)
in the latter end of the seventeenth year (30:6)
thus ended the seventeenth year of the reign of the judges (35:12)
74 (Alma 35:13-44:24)
in the eighteenth year of the reign of the judges (35:13)
in the eighteenth year of the reign of the judges (43:3)
in the commencement of the eighteenth year (43:4)
thus ended the eighteenth year of the reign of the judges (44:24)
73 (Alma 45:1-49:30)
in the nineteenth year of the reign of the judges (45:2)

in the commencement of the nineteenth year of the reign of the judges (45:20)
until nearly the end of the nineteenth year of the reign of the judges (46:37)
in the latter end of the nineteenth year of the reign of the judges (48:2)
as I have said, in the latter end of the nineteenth year (48:21)
in the eleventh month of the nineteenth year, on the tenth day of the month (49:1)
thus ended the nineteenth year of the reign of the judges (49:29)
72 B.C. (Alma 50:1-16)
in the commencement of the twentieth year of the reign of the judges (1)
in that same year (15)
thus ended the twentieth year (16)
71 (Alma 50:17-23)
in the commencement of the twenty and first year of the reign of the judges (17)
in the twenty and first year of the reign of the judges (23)
70-69 (Alma 50:24)
the twenty and second year of the reign of the judges also ended
also the twenty and third year
68 (Alma 50:25-40)
in the commencement of the twenty and fourth year of the reign of the judges (25)
thus ended the twenty and fourth year of the reign of the judges (35)
in that same year (37)
did commence his reign in the end of the twenty and fourth year (40)
67 (Alma 51:1-37)

in the commencement of the twenty and fifth year of the reign of the judges (1)
having commenced the twenty and fifth year (1)
in the twenty and fifth year of the reign of the judges (12)
thus ended the twenty and fifth year of the reign of the judges (37)
66 B.C. (Alma 52:1-14)
in the twenty and sixth year...on the first morning of the first month (1)
in the ending of the twenty and sixth year of the reign of the judges (14)
65 (Alma 52:15-18)
in the twenty and seventh year of the reign of the judges (15)
in the latter end of the twenty and seventh year of the reign of the judges (18)
64 (Alma 52:19-53:23)
in the commencement of the twenty and eighth year (52:19)
in that year (53:7)
thus ended the twenty and eighth year of the reign of the judges (53:23)
63 (Alma 54:1-55:35)
in the commencement of the twenty and ninth year of the judges (54:1)
thus ended the twenty and ninth year of the reign of the judges (55:35)
62 (Alma 59:1-62:11)
in the thirtieth year of the reign of the judges (59:1)
thus ended the thirtieth year of the reign of the judges (62:11)
61 (Alma 62:12-41)
in the commencement of the thirty and first year of the reign of the judges (12)

thus ended the thirty and first year of the reign of the judges (39)
60-57 B.C. (Alma 62:42-52)
in the thirty and fifth year of the reign of the judges (52)
56 (Alma 63:1-3)
in the commencement of the thirty and sixth year of the reign of the judges (1)
thus ended the thirty and sixth year of the reign of the judges (3)
55 (Alma 63:4-6)
in the thirty and seventh year of the reign of the judges (4)
thus ended the thirty and seventh year (6)
54 (Alma 63:7-9)
in the thirty and eighth year (7)
in this year (9)
thus ended the thirty and eighth year (9)
53 (Alma 63:10-17)
in the thirty and ninth year of the reign of the judges (10)
in this year (13)
also in this year (14)
also in this same year (15)
thus ended the thirty and ninth year of the reign of the judges (16)

An Account of the Sons of Mosiah

91-81 (Alma 17:5-25:2)[11]
in the first year of the reign of the judges (17:6)
land of Ammonihah…destroyed (25:2)
81-77 (Alma 25:3-27:16)[12]
met Alma (27:16)

Epistle from Helaman

66 B.C. (Alma 56:7-20)
in the twenty and sixth year (7)
in the twenty and sixth year (9)
thus ended the twenty sixth year (20)
65-64 (Alma 56:20-57:5)
in the commencement of the twenty and seventh year (56:20)
in the second month of this year (56:27)
in the morning of the third day of the seventh month (56:42)
thus ended the twenty and eighth year of the reign of the judges (57:5)
63 (Alma 57:6-58:41)
in the commencement of the twenty and ninth year (57:6)
this is the twenty and ninth year, in the latter end (58:38)
62 (Alma 56:1)
in the commencement of the thirtieth year of the reign of the judges, on the second day in the first month

Book of Helaman

52 B.C. (Helaman 1:1-13)
in the commencement of the fortieth year of the reign of the judges (1)
all this was done in the fortieth year of the reign of the judges; and it had an end (13)
51 (Helaman 1:14-34)
in the forty and first year of the reign of the judges (14)
thus ended the forty and first year of the reign of the judges (34)
50 (Helaman 2:1-14)
in the forty and second year of the reign of the judges (1)
thus ended the forty and second year of the reign of the judges (12)
49 (Helaman 3:1)
in the forty and third year of the reign of the judges
in the ending of the forty and third year
48 (Helaman 3:2)
in the forty and fourth year
47 (Helaman 3:2)
in the forty and fifth year
46 (Helaman 3:3-18)
in the forty and sixth (3)
the forty and sixth year of the reign of the judges ended (18)
45-44 (Helaman 3:19-22)
even in the forty and seventh year, and also in the forty and eighth year (19)
in the latter end of the forty and eighth year of the reign of the judges (22)
43 (Helaman 3:23-32)
in the forty and ninth year of the reign of the judges (23)
in this same year (24)
in this year (31)

in the remainder of the forty and ninth year (32)
42 B.C. (Helaman 3:32)
in the fiftieth year of the reign of the judges
41 (Helaman 3:33-35)
in the fifty and first year of the reign of the judges (33)
40 (Helaman 3:36)
the fifty and second year ended
39 (Helaman 3:37)
in the fifty and third year of the reign of the judges
38-37 (Helaman 4:1-3)
in the fifty and fourth year (1)
36 (Helaman 4:4)
in the fifty and sixth year of the reign of the judges
they were all that year
35 (Helaman 4:5)
in the fifty and seventh year
34-33 (Helaman 4:5-8)
in the fifty and eighth year of the reign of the judges (5)
all this was done in the fifty and eighth and ninth years of the reign of the judges (8)
32 (Helaman 4:9)
in the sixtieth year of the reign of the judges
31 (Helaman 4:10-17)
in the sixty and first year of the reign of the judges (10)
thus ended the sixty and first year of the reign of the judges (17)
30 (Helaman 4:18-6:1)
in the sixty and second year of the reign of the judges (4:18)
in this same year (5:1)
29 (Helaman 6:1-6)
when the sixty and second year of the reign of the judges had ended (1)
thus ended the sixty and third year (6)

28 B.C. (Helaman 6:7-13)
thus the sixty and fourth year did pass away (13)
27 (Helaman 6:14)
in the sixty and fifth year
thus passed away the sixty and fifth year
26 (Helaman 6:15)
in the sixty and sixth year of the reign of the judges
in the same year
thus ended the sixty and sixth year
25 (Helaman 6:16-32)
in the commencement of the sixty and seventh year (16)
it had come unto them in the sixty and seventh year of the reign of the judges (32)
24 (Helaman 6:33-41)
in the sixty and eighth year also (33)
thus ended the sixty and eighth year of the reign of the judges (41)
23-21 (Helaman 7:1-10:19)
in the sixty and ninth year of the reign of the judges (7:1)
thus ended the seventy and first year of the reign of the judges (10:19)
20 (Helaman 11:1-2)
in the seventy and second year of reign of the judges (1)
did last all that year (2)
19 (Helaman 11:2-5)
in the seventy and third year (2)
in this year (3)
18 (Helaman 11:5)
thus in the seventy and fourth year
17 (Helaman 11:6-16)
did also continue in the seventy and fifth year (6)
16 (Helaman 11:17-21)
in the seventy and sixth year (17)
the seventy and sixth year did end (21)

15 B.C. (Helaman 11:21)
the seventy and seventh year began
thus ended the seventy and seventh year
14 (Helaman 11:22)
in the seventy and eighth year
13 (Helaman 11:23)
in the seventy and ninth year
in that same year
12 (Helaman 11:24-29)
in the eightieth year of the reign of the judges (24)
in that same year (29)
thus ended the eightieth year of the reign of the judges (29)
11 (Helaman 11:30-35)
in the commencement of the eighty and first year (30)
thus ended this year (32)
thus ended the eighty and first year of the reign of the judges (35)
10 (Helaman 11:36)
in the eighty and second year
9 (Helaman 11:36)
in the eighty and third year
8 (Helaman 11:36)
in the eighty and fourth year
7 (Helaman 11:37-38)
in the eighty and fifth year (37)
thus ended the eighty and fifth year (38)
6 (Helaman 13:1-16:9)[13]
in the eighty and sixth year (13:1)
in this year (13:2)
thus ended the eighty and sixth year of the reign of the judges (16:9)
5 (Helaman 16:10)
thus ended also the eighty and seventh year of the reign

of the judges
4 B.C. (Helaman 16:11)
in the eighty and eighth year of the reign of the judges
3 (Helaman 16:12)
in the eighty and ninth year of the reign of the judges
2 (Helaman 16:13-25)
in the ninetieth year of the reign of the judges (13)
thus in this year (14)
thus ended the ninetieth year of the reign of the judges (24)

Third Nephi

1 B.C. (3 Nephi 1:1-14)[14]
the ninety and first year had passed away (1)
it was six hundred years from the time that Lehi left Jerusalem (1)
in the commencement of the ninety and second year (4)
this night shall the sign be given, and on the morrow come I into the world (13)
A.D. 1 (3 Nephi 1:15-26)[15]
they knew that it was the day that the Lord should be born (19)
in this same year (25)
thus the ninety and second year did pass away (26)
2 (3 Nephi 1:27)
the ninety and third year did also pass away
3-4 (3 Nephi 1:28-2:1)
in the ninety and fourth year (1:28)
thus passed away the ninety and fifth year also (2:1)
5 (3 Nephi 2:1-4)
thus did pass away the ninety and sixth year (4)
9 (3 Nephi 2:5-8)
an hundred years had passed away since the days of Mosiah (5)
six hundred and nine years had passed away since Lehi left Jerusalem (6)
nine years had passed away from the time when the sign was given (7)
nine years had passed away (8)
10 (3 Nephi 2:9-10)
thus passed away the tenth year also (10)
11 (3 Nephi 2:10)
the eleventh year also passed away

A.D. 13 (3 Nephi 2:11-16)
in the thirteenth year (11)
before this thirteenth year had passed away (13)
thus ended the thirteenth year (16)
14 (3 Nephi 2:17-18)
in the commencement of the fourteenth year (17)
thus ended the fourteenth year (18)
15 (3 Nephi 2:18-19)
in the fifteenth year (18)
thus ended the fifteenth year (19)
16 (3 Nephi 3:1-21)
in the sixteenth year (1)
17 (3 Nephi 3:22-26)
in the seventeenth year, in the latter end of the year (22)
18 (3 Nephi 4:1-4)
in the latter end of the eighteenth year (1)
thus the eighteenth year did pass away (4)
19 (3 Nephi 4:5-15)
in the nineteenth year (5)
in this year (6)
in the sixth month (7)
in this sixth month (11)
this nineteenth year did pass away (15)
20 (3 Nephi 4:15)
in the twenty year
21-25 (3 Nephi 4:16-5:8)
in the twenty and first year (4:16)
and thus had the twenty and second year passed away (5:7)
and the twenty and third year also (5:7)
and the twenty and fourth (5:7)
and the twenty and fifth (5:7)
and thus had twenty and five years passed away (5:7)
in the space of twenty and five years (5:8)

A.D. 26-27 (3 Nephi 6:1-4)
in the twenty and sixth year (1)
the twenty and sixth and seventh years passed away (4)
28 (3 Nephi 6:5-9)
thus passed away the twenty and eighth year (9)
29 (3 Nephi 6:10-14)
in the twenty and ninth year (10)
30 (3 Nephi 6:14-7:13)
in the thirtieth year (6:14)
in the commencement of the thirtieth year (6:17)
thus in the commencement of this, the thirtieth year (6:17)
did govern the people that year (6:19)
in this same year, yea, the thirtieth year (7:1)
thus ended the thirtieth year (7:13)
31 (3 Nephi 7:14-21)
in the thirty and first year (14)
in that same year (16)
the thirty and first year did pass away (21)
32 (3 Nephi 7:21-23)
thus passed away the thirty and second year also (23)
33 (3 Nephi 7:23-8:2)
in the commencement of the thirty and third year (7:23)
in the commencement of this year (7:26)
thus the more part of the year did pass away (7:26)
the thirty and third year had passed away (8:2)
34 (3 Nephi 8:3-26:16)[16]
in the thirty and fourth year, in the first month, on the fourth day (8:5)
in the ending of the thirty and fourth year (10:18)
the Lord truly did teach the people, for the space of three days (26:13)
on the morrow (26:16)

A.D. 34-35 (3 Nephi 26:17-28:16)
the thirty and forth year passed away, and also the thirty and fifth (4 Nephi 1:1)

Fourth Nephi

A.D. 36-37 (4 Nephi 1:1-4)
the thirty and fourth year passed away, and also the thirty and fifth (1)
in the thirty and sixth year (2)
the thirty and seventh year passed away also (4)
38 (4 Nephi 1:4-6)
thus did the thirty and eighth year passed away (6)
60-71 (4 Nephi 1:6-14)
even until the fifty and nine years had passed away (6)
the seventy and first year passed away (14)
101-110 (4 Nephi 1:14-18)
even an hundred years had passed away (14)
until an hundred and ten years had passed away (18)
111-194 (4 Nephi 1:18-21)
an hundred and ninety and four years from the coming of Christ (21)
201 (4 Nephi 1:21-24)
two hundred years had passed away (22)
in this two hundred and first year (24)
201-210 (4 Nephi 1:25-26)
211-230 (4 Nephi 1:27-34)
when two hundred and ten years had passed away (27)
even until two hundred and thirty years had passed away (34)
231-244 (4 Nephi 1:35-40)
in this year, yea, in the two hundred and thirty and first year (35)
in this year there arose (36)
two hundred and forty and four years had passed away (40)
245-250 (4 Nephi 1:40-41)
thus did two hundred and fifty years passed away (41)

A.D. 261-300 (4 Nephi 1:41-44)
and also two hundred and sixty years (41)
301-305 (4 Nephi 1:45-46)
when three hundred years had passed away (45)
306 (4 Nephi 1:47)
after three hundred and five years had passed away
321 (4 Nephi 1:48-49)
when three hundred and twenty years had passed away (48)
even until the three hundred and twentieth year from the coming of Christ (48)

Book of Mormon

A.D. 321 (Mormon 1:2-5)
about the time that Ammaron hid up the records (2)
I being about ten years of age (2)
322 (Mormon 1:6-11)
I, being eleven years old (6)
in this year (8)
in this same year (11)
322-326 (Mormon 1:12-14)
for the space of about four years (12)
326 (Mormon 1:15-2:2)
I, being fifteen years of age (1:15)
in that same year (2:1)
in my sixteenth year (2:2)
three hundred and twenty six years had passed away (2:2)
327-330 (Mormon 2:3-9)
in the three hundred and twenty and seventh year (3)
three hundred and thirty years had passed away (9)
331-344 (Mormon 2:10-15)
thus three hundred and forty and four years had passed away (15)
345 (Mormon 2:16, 20-21)
in the three hundred and forty and fifth year (16)
in this year (20)
346-349 (Mormon 2:22-28)
in the three hundred and forty and sixth year (22)
the three hundred and forty and ninth year had passed away (28)
350 (Mormon 2:28-29)
in the three hundred and fiftieth year (28)
350-360 (Mormon 3:1-3)
until ten years more had passed away (1)

A.D. 360 (Mormon 3:4-6)
after this tenth year had passed away, making, in the whole, three hundred and sixty years from the coming of Christ (4)
361 (Mormon 3:7)
in the three hundred and sixty and first year
in that year
362 (Mormon 3:8-22)
in the three hundred and sixty and second year (8)
363 (Mormon 4:1-6)
in the three hundred and sixty and third year (1)
364-366 (Mormon 4:7-10)
in the three hundred and sixty and fourth year (7)
the three hundred and sixty and sixth year had passed away (10)
367 (Mormon 4:10-15)
in the three hundred and sixty and seventh year (15)
367-375 (Mormon 4:16)
until the three hundred and seventy and fifth year
375-379 (Mormon 4:17-5:5)
in this year (4:17)
thus three hundred and seventy and nine years passed away (5:5)
380-384 (Mormon 5:6-6:5)
in the three hundred and eightieth year (5:6)
when three hundred and eighty and four years had passed away (6:5)
385 (Mormon 6:6-7:10)
401 (Mormon 8:1-9:37)
four hundred year have passed away since the coming of our Lord and Savoir (8:6)

Words of Mormon

A.D. 385 (Words of Mormon 1:1-9, 11)

I have witnessed almost all the destruction of my people (1)
I deliver these plates into the hands of my son (2)
I, Mormon, proceed to finish out my record (9)

Book of Moroni

421 A.D. (Moroni 1)
34 (Moroni 2-5)[17]
350-360 (Moroni 6-7)[18]
About 380 (Moroni 8-9)[19]
421 (Moroni 10)
more than four hundred and twenty years have passed away since the sign was given of the coming of Christ (1)

Conclusion

The internal chronology of the Book of Mormon never misses a beat: over three hundred references, and they are all kept in harmony with each other. The Book of Mormon is not a collection of campfire stories. Mormon had been entrusted with the historical records of his people. The Book of Mormon is an abridgment of the record of the people of Nephi. Mormon had the dates because the large plates of Nephi were full of them.

Notes

[1] Mormon recorded of the time of Christ: "the ninety and first year [of the reign of the judges] had passed away and it was six hundred years from the time that Lehi left Jerusalem" (3 Nephi 1:1). In other words, ninety-one years had passed away since the days of Mosiah, six hundred years had passed away since Lehi left Jerusalem (see 3 Nephi 2:5-7), and the sign of Christ's birth was yet to be given. It was the latter part of 1 B.C. By adding back six hundred years, Lehi left Jerusalem in 601 B.C.

Although Lehi left Jerusalem in the latter part of 601, the majority of the first year of the Lehi calendar would have taken place in 600 B.C.

[2] Lehi came out of Jerusalem in the first year of the reign of Zedekiah (see preface for Third Nephi). After eight years in the wilderness, it would have been the ninth year of the reign of Zedekiah. At this time Nephi was teaching: "they have become wicked, yea, nearly unto ripeness; and I know not but they are at this day about to be destroyed" (1 Nephi 17:43). According to the Old Testament, Jerusalem was destroyed in the eleventh year of king Zedekiah (2 King 25:2; Jeremiah 52:5).

[3] Nephi began the use of the phrase "years had passed away." Those who followed him also used this phrase. At the moment when thirty years had passed away, it would have been in the latter part of 571 B.C., but the majority of the thirty and first year would have taken place in 570 B.C.

[4] The last event that Amaleki mentions before delivering up the small plates was "king Benjamin did drive [the Lamanites] out of the land of Zarahemla" (Omni 1:24). This peace was established before the birth of Mosiah, who was born in 154 B.C. (Mosiah 1:1-2; 29:46).

[5] Mormon usually began each book in the Book of Mormon with a preface. As the Nephite nation drew nearer to its close, those prefaces became smaller. Mormon also began each book by referring to the year the events were taking place. The book of Mosiah does not follow either of these standards. Also, the book of Mosiah does not begin with material about Mosiah, it begins with king Benjamin. In the printer's manuscript of the Book of Mormon, the first chapter of the book of Mosiah started with a Roman numeral III, which was corrected by crossing out the last two of the Roman

numerals. This has led some scholars to suggest that "the first two chapters of the book of Mosiah were among the 116 pages lost by Martin Harris" (Grant Hardy ed., *The Book of Mormon, A Reader's Edition* (2003), 177). If the first part of the book of Mosiah was lost, then this book may have been named for the Mosiah who led his people from the land of Nephi to the land of Zarahemla in about 200 B.C.

[6] Mosiah was born in 154 B.C. He died in 91 B.C., "being sixty and three years old" (Mosiah 29:46).

[7] Mormon viewed things in calendar years. A good example of this can be found in the first verse of the book of Alma: "in the first year of the reign of the judges over the people of Nephi." The majority of the first calendar year of the reign of the judges took place in 91 B.C.

The reign of king Mosiah began "about four hundred and seventy-six years from the time Lehi left Jerusalem" (Mosiah 6:4), or in the four hundred and seventy-seventh year of the Lehi calendar, which most closely corresponds to 124 B.C.

Mormon confirmed this date when he gave the history of the five hundred and tenth year of the Lehi calendar, or in the first year of the reign of the judges, which most closely corresponds to 91 B.C. In this year king Mosiah died, in the thirty-third year of his reign (Mosiah 29:46). By taking the year 91 B.C. and adding back the thirty-three years of his reign, we can calculate that his reign began in 124 B.C.

[8] The sons of Mosiah took their journey into the wilderness "in the first year of the judges" (Alma 17:6), which most closely corresponds to 91 B.C.

[9] Alma and the people of the Lord likely arrived in the land of Zarahemla in 121 B.C., shortly after the people of Limhi. After Ammon found the people of king Limhi, they were desirous to be baptized (Mosiah 21:33). After their arrival in the land of Zarahemla, they would have immediately expressed a desire to be baptized. Mormon recorded that after king Mosiah had gathered all the people, Alma taught the people, and "king Limhi was desirous that he might be baptized; and all his people were desirous that they might be baptized also" (Mosiah 25:17). Alma and the people of the Lord must have returned shortly after the people of Limhi, or the people of Limhi would have already been baptized by someone other than Alma.

[10] Mathematically, if you subtract from the number ninety-two, the year of the reign of the judges, you have the year B.C.
[11] The land of Ammonihah was destroyed "in the eleventh year of the reign of the judges," or in 81 B.C. (Alma 16:1-3).
[12] The sons of Mosiah began their journey to the land of Nephi in the first year of the judges (Alma 17:6). They taught "the word of God for the space of fourteen years among the Lamanites" (Alma 17:4). By subtracting fourteen from the first year of the judges, or 91 B.C., we can confirm that the first few verses of the seventeenth chapter of Alma took place in 77 B.C.
[13] Samuel the Lamanite, prophesied: "Behold, I give unto you a sign; for five years more cometh, and behold, then cometh the Son of God to redeem all those who shall believe on his name. And behold, this will I give unto you for a sign at the time of his coming; for behold, there shall be great lights in heaven, insomuch that in the night before he cometh there shall be no darkness, insomuch that it shall appear unto man as if it was day. Therefore, there shall be one day and a night and a day, as if it were one day and there were no night; and this shall be unto you for a sign; for ye shall know of the rising of the sun and also of its setting; therefore they shall know of a surety that there shall be two days and a night; nevertheless the night shall not be darkened; and it shall be the night before he is born. And behold, there shall a new star arise, such an one as ye never have beheld; and this also shall be a sign unto you" (Helaman 14:2-5). This prophecy was given in the eighty-sixth year of the reign of the judges. This year most closely corresponds to 6 B.C. But it is important to remember that the eighty-sixth year actually began in the latter part of 7 B.C., and we do not know when in this year Samuel made this prophecy. Actually, either of these years could explain why "there were some who began to say that the time was past for the words to be fulfilled, which were spoken by Samuel, the Lamanite" (3 Nephi 1:6). For if we take even five years from 6 B.C., we still have 1 B.C., possibly months before the sign would be given. Samuel said, "five years more cometh, and behold, then cometh the Son of God" (Helaman 14:2). We now know that five years did come, and the sixth year did not come, before the Son of God came into the world.
[14] In order for the six hundredth year of the Lehi calendar to end between the ending of the ninety-first and the beginning of ninety-

second year of the reign of the judges, these two calendars had to end at the same time. This implies that they were in synchronization with each other, that Mosiah's death did not mark the beginning of the first day of the first month of a new Nephite calendar.
[15] Mormon wrote, "And nine years had passed away from the time when the sign was given, which was spoken by the prophets, that Christ should come into the world. Now the Nephites began to reckon their time from this period when the sign was given, or from the coming of Christ; therefore, nine years had passed away" (3 Nephi 2:7-8). Some scholars suggest that the Nephite calendar was shifted or adjusted at this time to begin at the sign of Christ's birth (John P. Pratt, "Book of Mormon Chronology," *Encyclopedia of Mormonism* (1992), 1:171). In other words, the sign of Christ's birth became the first day of the first month of a new Nephite calendar.
[16] If the Nephite calendar had been shifted or adjusted to begin at the sign of Christ's birth, then Christ died at the age of thirty-three years and three days. If the calendar was not adjusted, then he lived less than thirty-three years.

Jesus Christ did not immediately show himself unto the people of Nephi. Mormon recorded that the signs of his death came in first month of the thirty-fourth year (3 Nephi 8:5), and that he did not manifest himself unto them until "the ending of the thirty and fourth year" (3 Nephi 10:18).
[17] Statements like "words of Christ, which he spake unto his disciples" (Moroni 2:1), or "the manner which the disciples, who were called the elders of the church, ordained priests and teachers" (Moroni 3:1), or "according to the commandments of Christ" (Moroni 4:1), suggest that these documents were from the time of Christ.
[18] In A.D. 350, a treaty was made between the Nephites and the Lamanites which lasted ten years. During this time Mormon was commanded to begin his ministry (Mormon 3:2). Mormon would have given sermons, and baptisms would have been performed. This ten-year period is the most likely time for these two chapters.
[19] Mormon wrote his first epistle soon after his son had been called to the ministry (Moroni 8:1). In it he promised, "I will write again" (Moroni 8:27). Mormon began his second epistle by stating, "I write unto you again" (Moroni 9:1). These epistles were not years apart. They mention each other. They were a pair.

Mormon served in the military at two different times: first, from A.D. 326 to 362; second, from about 375 to 385. It is difficult to believe that Mormon's epistles are from the first period. Mormon wrote in his second epistle of the Nephite's thrist for blood and revenge (Moroni 9:5, 23). Mormon had left the military in 362 because of the Nephites' plan for vengeance (Mormon 3:9-11). It is also difficult to believe that Moroni would have been old enough to be called to the ministry until some time after the first period.

When we review the second period, from the time Mormon took command of the armies, for "a sore battle" in which the Nephites "did not conquer" (Moroni 9:2), we find only two. First is the battle that started in A.D. 380 (Mormon 5:6-7). The second is the last great battle in A.D. 385. Mormon and Moroni were together at Cumorah. Because only twenty-four Nephites survived the last great battle, it is difficult to believe that Mormon's second epistle was written at that late date (Moroni 9:3, 17, 22-24). This epistle was most likely written shortly after the battle that began in 380.

Index

H

J

L

M

N

P